an unlikely catlady

feral adventures in the backyard jungle

NINA MALKIN

The Lyons Press
Guilford, Connecticut
An imprint of The Globe Pequot Press

Page v: **CRAZY** © 1961 Sony/ATV Songs LLC. All rights administered by Sony/ATV Music
Publishing 8 Music Square West, Nashville TN 37203. All rights reserved. Used by permission.

The Lyons Press is an imprint of The Globe Pequot Press
10   9   8   7   6   5   4   3   2   1

Printed in the United States of America

ISBN-13: 978-1-59228-972-1
ISBN-10: 1-59228-972-X
Library of Congress Cataloging-in-Publication Data

Malkin, Nina.
    An unlikely cat lady : feral adventures in the backyard jungle / Nina Malkin.
       p. cm.
    ISBN-13: 978-1-59228-972-1
    ISBN-10: 1-59228-972-X
  1. Feral cats—New York (State)—New York—Anecdotes. 2. Urban animals—New York
(State)—New York—Anecdotes. 3. Malkin, Nina. 4. Brooklyn (New York, N.Y.) I. Title.
    SF450.M35 2007
    636.8092—dc22

                                                                                    2006022385

"I'm crazy for trying and crazy for crying and I'm crazy for loving you . . ."

—Willie Nelson, "Crazy"

Dedicated to the memory of

Janice Dorner

contents

preface

this is a true story about

cats. And people. Cats and people; cats and cats; people and people. Basically this is a story about relationships. And love and loss, life and death, fear and loathing. Community, compassion and obsession. Sex, drugs, and rock 'n' roll. A place, a time, an age. But, mostly, cats . . .

The feral cat situation worldwide is serious. Some would use the word *crisis* or *epidemic*, but I don't want to seem hysterical. Since my involvement with ferals began I've been hyperaware of coming off like a lunatic—one of those crazy cat ladies. Yet conservative estimates put the feral cat population at ten million in the continental United States alone, and the number might be as high as ten times that. That's a lot of cats being born, getting sick, and dropping dead; they are the great unwanted (but not unwashed—even homeless and destitute, they are notoriously finicky about grooming). I read somewhere that a pair of breeding cats and their offspring can exponentially produce more than four hundred thousand of their kind in seven years.

But forget the figures for a second, and consider the breadth of the problem. Feral cats are everywhere. From the mountains to the prairies to the oceans white with foam. Every town, village, hamlet, and burg has a feral cat situation. Your town has one. So does mine, Brooklyn, New York. Maybe you'd think any kind of critter trouble would peak out in the country—that in urban areas feral cats would be supplanted, by a process of natural selection, to make room for more closets. A logical assumption, but no. If you've got Dumpsters, or garbage cans, or litterbugs, you've got ferals. You can't starve them into extinction; the hungrier they get, the more vehemently nature seems to deliver the message: *Breed! Breed! Breed!* You can't effectively kill 'em off, either. Euthanasia, rat poison, automatic weapons have all been employed to little avail; live cats miraculously take the place of dead ones. The only solution, experts contend, is a three-pronged approach called trap-neuter-return (TNR).

It's simple! Catch cat. Fix cat. Let cat go as John Barry's "Born Free" swells in your mind and you fancy yourself a latter-day Joy Adamson. Repeat on all cats in immediate vicinity. Watch over cats for the rest of their or your natural lives.

Of course, TNR is a management solution, not a final solution. The main reason there are feral cats—cats one or more generations from domesticity—is people. It's true: Someone you know may acquire a cat only to become disillusioned upon learning that: (1) cats scratch; (2) cats shed; (3) cats urinate/defecate; (4) cats are not dogs. So this someone you know does the "Born Free" number without benefit of castration/hysterectomy, and ta-da! More cats. Needy yet nonchalant nobodies. The fast and the furriest. Cute, mangy, stupid, clever, rambunctious, ravenous. Territorial as Crips and Bloods combined. Black, orange, gray, white, tabby, calico, tortoiseshell inbred little bastards.

That said, my personal exposure to ferals is on a smaller scale. Much smaller. Single digits, okay. Five, give or take—never more than nine, and never even nine at a time. I don't have a situation. I don't even consider myself dealing with what's known in feral cat vernacular as a "colony." What I have is a family.

But, well, you know how families are . . .

chapter 1

laws *of* cattraction

brooklyn likes to brag about

its diversity. But Brooklyn is huge. Two-point-five million people huge. More souls than San Francisco, Boston, Atlanta, and St. Louis combined—just not necessarily in a blender. I know all about it—I'm a native, born and raised in one of Brooklyn's homogeneous zones, survivor of an adolescence that viewed *Saturday Night Fever* as cinema verité. That same area, my old hood, remains homogeneous—a whole different kind of homogeneous, a full-180 homogeneous, parallel-universe homogeneous. The tip of East Flatbush known as Flatlands was pretty much exclusively Jewish and Italian back then; today it could be called Little West Indies (and I doubt the proximity to Jamaica Bay has anything to do with it). Yet it was the promise of Brooklyn-as-melting-pot that brought me home—after thirteen years in Manhattan, interspersed by a seven-year hitch in LA—when I fell in love.

1

Jason Shealy Stutts was my boyfriend then, he's my husband now; we wanted to live together and figured, what the hell—let's mortgage ourselves up the wazoo and get a house. We wanted a brownstone, chockablock with original details like tin ceilings and hardwood floors, mantelpieces in every room. We also wanted what seemed to be a diametrically opposed domicile—one we could afford. But beyond charming touches and square footage and feasible down payments we wanted to live in a place where everyone looks different. That way, we'd be more likely to blend in. Don't be alarmed—I'm not the Nina the Bearded Lady, he's not the Jason the Fish-Head Boy—but most folks would consider us an unconventional couple. So we came house hunting here, to the borough of my birth, heeding Brooklyn's rainbow boast.

Well, we know there are parts of Brooklyn that are still all white because we looked there. We know there are sections that are still all black because we looked there, too. We didn't belong in those places. We found where we belong in Sunset Park—simply Sunset, to us locals—and if you take a walk around here you'll see why Brooklyn has bragging rights. Some people will tell you Sunset is largely Latin, or largely Chinese. I'm telling you that on our block every race, color, and creed except maybe Martian represents, plus all sorts of mix-and-mash cross-cultural pollinations as well.

Including, I am pleased to report, calico.

It's the day after Thanksgiving, and boy, am I thankful. Yesterday I fed a dozen people, with no runs to the emergency room. A big deal, since the turkey was in the oven seven hours and the juices refused to run clear. The juices, in fact, were running the color of cranberry juice. Pretty much the same color as the Code Red anxiety attack I valiantly sought to hold at bay. Among the guests was my new mother-in-law, Janelle, the sort of southern woman who makes everything from scratch, who not only owns Junior League cookbooks but contributes to them as well. This was the first time Janelle would eat something I'd prepared, and it was only Thanksgiving—aka The Most Important Meal of the Year. And let's be real: I'm a New York Jew, one year her junior and sixteen years older than her son, so probably not the daughter-in-law she always envisioned.

The planets of the culinary cosmos ultimately aligned in my favor after I cranked the oven to eleven. Half an hour later, better late than never, I pulled out the bird to find that the popper had not only popped, it had exploded, blackened. The meat thermometer was off the charts. And the juices? What juices, we don't need no stinking juices.

Was I thankful? Damn skippy. In fact, Thanksgiving was the icing on my cake of thankful. This had been a banner year for me. Not that I didn't have a life before—great guy, steady job, nice apartment, plus all the people I cared about were healthy. But this year my first-ever functional relationship led to the altar (well, City Hall), and I found my dream house. Yeah, it was all good. Dinner was served, with no casualties to report.

So now it's the following morning and I'm waiting for Jason, Janelle, and her husband, Mike, to get their act together. The plan is to walk to Bay Ridge—about a mile, or as we say in Brooklyn, "a coupla blocks"—get slabs of Sicilian at Gino's, then poke around the two Salvation Armies nearby. (Jason and I are big thrift-shoppers—there is little in our wardrobes, not to mention our arts and crap home decor, that wasn't gently broken in for us by others.) I'm chomping at the bit, so I wait outside, sitting on the stoop while in-laws arrange sweaters and scarves. Soon the stone steps chill my butt cheeks, so I get up to dispose of some of the advertising flyers that attach themselves to our iron gate like they're printed on magnets instead of paper, and . . . whoa! . . . hey! . . . holy crap! . . . what's that?

That!

There!

Idling by the curb a few houses down. It's small . . . tiny! Kind of brownish . . . sort of orange. Oh my goodness! Could it be . . . a cat? Such a gaspy heart-fluttery response, you'd think I just spied Jake Gyllenhaal licking his paw against the hubcap of a broke-down Monte Carlo. Yes indeed—I definitely detect a feline presence. My Jakeworthy reaction isn't so strange, really. I'm just surprised, that's all. A whole spring and summer have gone by here in Sunset and I never saw a single stray, either on the block or out in our backyard. Suddenly, with winter coming on, there's a poor little four-pawed street punk, washing her face, pretty as you please.

I do what comes naturally—prone as I am to "cattraction," a condition technically known as the feline effect (someday scientists will identify exactly what combination of brain chemicals produce this). I assume the position. Drop to one knee (it is a proposal, is it not?), extend one arm, fingers curved, and trill—not too softly, not too loud: "He-e-e-e-re, kitty, kitty, kitty!"

And she comes running, bounding, racing—not away from me but toward me—and leaps right into my arms.

I have a job. I work as an editor at a popular magazine for teenagers, so I am apt to say that a skirt or a purse or a lead singer is the cutest thing ever—it's an occupational hazard—but this little cat, no, really, she is the cutest thing ever. Her coat is a smudgy patchwork of black, rust, white, gray and an almost mauve—on closer inspection more tortoiseshell than calico—and while she weighs about as much as a pair of socks, she's petite in stature so carries skinny nicely. She is clean, but her fur is of the street, a bit bristly, recalling a cactus—not the rich chinchilla of Iggy and Echo, the two cats who concede to cohabitate with us, who have nothing better to do than preen eleven times a day. There's something gummy and exposed about her lower lip; it looks like a tangerine-pink pout or some kind of kitty gingivitis. This does not detract. She is a charmer.

"Look!" I present my new best friend to Jason, Janelle, and Mike, beaming like the middle school loser who snared, by divine providence or perhaps hidden agenda, the attention of the popular girl. In-laws half smile, bemused yet indulgent; husband reaches out a finger to give the little cat a chin chuck.

"Whurr'd you git the critter?" Jason is inclined to overdo his natural-born South Carolina twang in the presence of wildlife.

"She was right over there, and I called and she came running! Can you believe how sweet she is?" I press the cat onto Jason's chest. He (sucker!) doesn't hesitate, and she (slut!) doesn't, either. "Here, take her!"

Cat gives husband big golden goo-goo eyes. (Love at first sight for her, as it was for me. Who wouldn't tumble for his tardy schoolboy look—that floppy hair, lanky frame, and perpetually askew wire glasses? Well, somebody, I suppose. Somebody has to marry all those investment bankers.)

"How do you know she's a girl?"

Silly boy, he doesn't know tricolored cats are virtually always female. As I explain calico genetics, she wriggles around in his arms, not to get loose but to get in closer, tunnel his armpit, crawl inside his pocket if possible, really sink her hooks. She is vibrating with joy. And so am I. "Just hold her while I go get some food," I say, then turn to Janelle and Mike, head bobbling: "I'm going to get some food!"

"Nina . . . ," Jason calls to my wake.

"It'll take two seconds!" I promise.

I put down the kibble; Jason puts down the cat. She springs for the bowl, yet glances up every other gobbled bite to ensure we're still there. I'm the village idiot, positively pixilated, dream-swoggled, entranced: *Look at her! Look at her eating! Look at her looking at us!* Janelle doesn't quite comprehend, but she would if the cat were a dog—her big mutt Betsey was a follow-home. Mike doesn't get it at all—but he's married to Janelle so understands that womenfolk can be like that about animals. As he wonders if we're going to stand around watching a cat eat kibble all day, his battened-down impatience curling up at the flaps, Jason takes my elbow and I understand I'm expected to move, tear myself away and proceed with our plan—pizzeria, thrift store, secondary thrift store—and yeah, sure, I can do that, I can control the feline effect and function like any other normal human being. As we make our way to the avenue, I only look back over my shoulder once.

chapter 2

bastards *of* young

i am **not** one of those people.

You know what I mean. Those crazy cat people. Nope, not me. I'm just a normal, ordinary gal who likes to have another species around. It keeps human hubris to a minimum, and it's as close as you can get to living with a cartoon character. Besides, I profess to appreciate all animals except maybe monkeys (I mean, who needs monkeys when we've got all these human beings?). Cats may be my species of choice, but that's due more to practicality than anything else. After all, one cannot comfortably keep a pony in a one-bedroom apartment. Nor, as Harlem resident Antoine Yates was to learn, a four-hundred-pound Bengal tiger and a five-foot alligator cousin known as a caiman.

A cat is small, compact, and convincingly gives off an impression of independence, the ideal animal companion for a generally selfish person such as myself. Which is to say I'm not a cat accumulator, never was. You could come to my place and sit down wherever you wished without worrying about landing on or otherwise pissing off a cat. Except one. For two decades I was a one-cat woman. Whoopie was with me through six apartments, both coasts, and a wide assortment of gentlemen callers.

Today there is a balanced human-to-feline ratio in our home. One boy, one girl human: One boy, one girl feline. The fact that some cat-related curios, tchotchkes, and dubious objets d'art are scattered about the joint cannot be held against me because there are so many other curios, tchotchkes, and dubious objets d'art that the random cat paint-by-numbers or figurine doesn't even stand out.

Jason is not a crazy cat person, either. As a matter of fact, he was a latecomer to cats. Jason grew up in the country; he grew up with dogs. Dogs you could depend on for huntin' and fishin' and such. You gave a dog a name because you called the name and the dog came apace, tail wagging. Cats were things that lived in the barn and didn't have names; cats were rodent control.

However, when Jason was wooing me he cannily wooed Whoopie as well. His bending over backward to befriend her endeared him to me greatly, and when she eventually took to him—the only person besides me she would let hold her—it was clear he was The One. Who knew Whoopie was the love litmus test, the man swami? I might have saved myself a lot of heartache over the years if I'd just thrown my cat on some of cads I dragged home. Not only did Whoopie abide Jason, the two of them forged a genuine connection her final years on this earth. Of course, she was about 140 in cat years and perhaps too feeble and senile to rebuff him, but by then—too bad, cat—I was hooked.

If Jason reached out to Whoopie as romantic subterfuge, Iggy and Echo he loves unconditionally. What's not to love—they are extraordinary, as individuals but especially as a pair. They are brother and sister, yin and yang, Ho Ho and Twinkie. Iggy (aka Ignoramus, Ramos, Ignatz, Popi), with his shiny black tuxedo and fluffy white shirtfront, and Echo (aka Alien Baby, Stinkerbelle, Tha Vanilla Killa), with her sleek white gown and black cloverleaf cap, tail, and left-flank ink spot. He is a great big bucket of love who nuzzles complete strangers. She is a tease, a flirt, a coquette— but a clever one, smart enough to found a chapter of feline Mensa.

Jason is so besotted with the two of them I can get a little jealous. He cannot retire at night without scooping them both up in his arms and bringing them to our bed, nor arise without morning cat worship. He can't leave the house without doing a cat scan—ensuring they're diligently at work holding down pieces of furniture and kissing them adieu. He plays with them tirelessly, composes pop songs in their honor, clips their claws conscientiously, and is a regular Captain Queeg about their poop deck. Personally, I'd let the box go awhile but Jason wouldn't dream of exposing his beloveds to stinky litter. And then there's his treasure chest—a velvet-lined rosewood box for the safekeeping of shed whiskers.

Devoted? To be sure. A little OCD? Maybe. But crazy? Nah. Not Jason. Not me. Iggy and Echo are special. They're *ours*. Other cats are . . . well, they're nice enough, aesthetically pleasing, no reason not to give them a rub and a tickle, but other cats are just that, other cats. As in, not ours. Yet there's a plane between *ours* and *other*, and that's the milieu of the amicable stray—a cat who's yours, mine, anybody's.

We call her Flaca. Jason picks the name. *Flaco* is Spanish for "skinny"; *Flaca* the feminized version. Jason has Spanish on the brain; he and Mr. Felipe down the block have been swapping words and phrases in an informal, neighborly SSL/ESL exchange program. It's nice that Jason's taking an interest in my new hobby, when other husbands would be putting their foot down and shaking their fist about feeding another cat when we've already got two. So Flaca it is.

For about a week and a half.

Every morning Flaca either waits at our gate, weaving in and out of its wrought-iron ribs, or soaks up a spot of too-warm-to-be-December sunshine between our stoop and Mr. Felipe's. If I don't see her, I'll start down the street, pss-pss-pssing and spewing that obnoxious puckering noise I won't even begin to try to spell, and up she'll sprint, tail a mast, paws landing in the straight-line saunter runway models imitate, with a high-pitched mew of salutation. It's not a big thrill to see her, just an ordinary, everyday, average little thrill, a thimbleful of thrill, a thrill nugget. It's a fleeting thrill, too, that may only last till I reach the subway and someone gets in my face or steps on my shoe. Best of all it's a selfish thrill—mine, mine, all mine. Not that anyone else wants it.

I scoop her up, scold her for making me late to work, and put her through her gymnastic routine. Flaca is one of those elastic cats who'll contort into all manner of poses in my arms and on my lap. Maybe we should have called her Gumby. This do-what-you-will-with-me attitude is commonly found in felines with a touch of canine in them. Iggy, for instance. Iggy's not as limber as Flaca, his moves wouldn't give Bela Karolyi a hard-on, but he likes being picked up and toted about because damn, it sure beats walking. Iggy is one lazy mofo (he has a touch of sloth in him, too). Echo on the other hand is pure cat and considers such conduct undignified. She approves of petting (when she wants to be petted, which is usually around four in the morning). She also has a masochistic fetish for having her tail pulled. But she will not—will *not!*—submit to being held. I pretty much accept this, though Jason is forever grabbing her, sure she'll come to her senses. A pipe dream—and Jason bears the scratches to show for it.

A street cat, an urchin who never knows where her next kick is coming from, ought to be more cautious, but Flaca's as floppy and amenable as a hooker on quaaludes. Hence Jason's theory that she belongs to someone. Or belonged. That she either got lost, or got tossed. There aren't any MISSING CAT posters stapled to telephone poles in the hood, and I'm incensed that someone would throw away a perfectly good cat. Soon the weather will get a wake-up call from the calendar and turn cold. I haven't said boo about taking Flaca in since—really, truly—I don't want to. I'm happy with the cat–person equanimity in our home. I'm afraid to set a precedent. As a crap collector, I know that's how it starts—take one, take in every one that crosses your line of vision. It's bad enough with inanimate objects. Cats? Better not. Yet I do start musing on Flaca's future: Should I put up FOUND CAT signage? Ask around for anyone who might want to offer refuge?

Before I can do either, Flaca is gone. Without so much as an *adios amiga.* One day she's there, the next she's not. My mind spits out cause of death scenarios worthy of *Law & Order*: death by SUV, death by fledgling psychopath, death by slavering wildebeest.

Jason's a bright-sider. "She's such a nice little cat, I bet somebody took her in," he reasons.

Could be. If Flaca were any more sociable, she'd have her own cat chat show on Lifetime. So I hope Jason's right. I also hope he'll ignore my sulky malaise, because I'm a grown woman and shouldn't be sniffling like a four-year-old. But I am. I do. I do feel abandoned; I do feel sad. I do head out in the morning wishing she'll be there, and I do get disappointed when she's not. The mystery makes it harder. If I knew for certain a sweet old lady was giving Flaca sateen cushions to claw and saucers of milk to slurp in some cozy parlor right now, I'd be fine. But I don't know that, and the not knowing hurts. Flaca's vanishing act would be Twilight Zoney if it didn't make stone-cold sense that she'd drop dead from unnatural causes and get swept into oblivion or the corner sewer by one of those sanitation vehicles with the whirling circular brushes that lumber down the street, big, blind, and moaning like a diabetic mastodon.

Flaca is a speck, a smidgen, a piss-ant, a piss-off, nobody, nobody's, nothing.

I try to shake off the sulk. Tell myself: She's not *your* cat. She's a stray. Hence the term. Quit bellyaching. There are two lovely felines holding down pieces of furniture right here in the living room. Here, Iggy! Here, Echo! Show Mama some love. But I wonder: Could Flaca's bounce be my karma for greed, my wanting more cat and not knowing when enough cat is enough cat? This is not good—I'm getting metaphysical. Somebody stop me before I start chanting the Meow Mix jingle as a mantra, murmuring Hail Basts of atonement.

Somebody does. The following Saturday afternoon somebody has me going, "Flaca? Flaca who?"

Banal routine is vastly underrated. No one sings the praises of banal routine, at least not publicly, probably because it's banal, and it's routine, and next to exciting adventure it doesn't look so good, at least not in print or cocktail-party conversation. But I'm not afraid to champion banal routine. Knowing what you're going to do, and when you're going to do it, and that it won't be especially taxing, physically or mentally—you can't beat that with a billy club. People like to say, "I love a challenge!" Usually they are saying it at a job interview or on an audition tape for a reality television show. Me, personally, I hate a challenge. This is not a symptom of aging. I've always preferred to do what came easily and enjoyably. Anything requiring hand–eye coordination got ruled out early. Ditto for anything requiring arithmetic. I just want to do what I want to do, what I do marginally well, and when I can't I cast my vote for banal routine over difficult ordeal every time.

Saturdays are devoted to banal routine. Wake up for extended daily cat worship, followed by yoga. Purchase doughnut holes from Dunkin' Donuts; conduct Sunset Park Writers' Collective at local library (writers in the collective are between the ages of ten and eighteen, and while there are occasional spasms of surprise and delight, let's be real, there's nothing more predictably banal than adolescent poetry), read, write, eat doughnut holes. Fetch Jason, go for lunch at George's (coffee shop) or Cinco Estrella (excellent, authentic Mexican food, although the language barrier ultimately means every order arrives askew, with at least one item missing and one you didn't ask for in its place). After lunch, go home, crank tunes, clean house. We are up to the housecleaning part when Jason, distracted from the mountain of laundry he's ostensibly folding, summons me into the bedroom. "You're little friend is back," he says. "And she's not alone . . ."

I drop my mop and fly to the bedroom window. I am quickly transfixed.

"That's not Flaca . . . ," I say.

Flaca is—was—a tortoiseshell. This is a tabby. And this tabby is leading four biscuit-sized kittens in a stray cat strut through the run-amok weeds, ruined railings, and long-forgotten Big Wheels of the property behind the commercial buildings on Brooklyn's Fifth Avenue, and straight into our backyard.

I give Jason (irony intended) puppy-dog eyes. But what is he going to say anyway? *No wife of mine is dashing outside in her sweatpants and slippers to give away our hard-earned cat food.* He's not immune to the forces of cattraction. He follows me down to the kitchen.

"What's going on here? I don't understand," I mumble on descent. "Spring and summer—that's kitten season. It's practically winter; it doesn't make sense." I reach the pantry, fill two bowls, then hit the sink for water. A veritable flurry of activity. "They'll probably just run away," I tell Jason on the way out the back door.

But they don't.

At the sound of the door they freeze. Mama Cat freezes; baby cat bumps into Mama's rump and freezes; other baby cats bump into one another's rumps and freeze exponentially. Jason and I venture into the yard, and a pas de deux ensues, except it's not a pas de deux, there are five of them, two of us, you do the math. We crouch, we creep, make beckoning noises. The family encroaches. We take a few steps back; they take a few steps closer. The tabby is hunched, tail low, shoulders raised. She's scrawny. Nursing a brood of four has got to take a lot out of a cat.

What does it mean to be ravenous? During the 1980s I dabbled in bulimia; I know what it is to be ravenous emotionally. But ravenous, literally ravenous—what is that? Not just ravenous but at the same time unable to charge and devour when food is proffered. Instead being suspicious of the food, the source of the food, and every unseen squeak or thump or crackle within a fifty-yard radius that potentially threatens the food, or threatens you—threatens to turn the diner into dinner. Slowly, finally, she makes it to the bowl and begins to mitigate the hunger.

Her kittens appear to be six to eight weeks old—each about the size of my fist, eyes still blue, covered in coronas of dandelion fluff—scarcely old enough for solid eats but eager to investigate. Two are twins, white with tabby splotches, except one has a white face while the other wears a patterned mask. There's a white kitten with gray splotches and a rheumy, marble eye, no doubt blind. And there's a runt, black and white, who keeps getting nudged off the chow by more aggressive siblings.

Jason and I, silent and still, watch until it's no longer possible to be silent and still. I don't know which of us cracks first, but one of us moves, makes a sound, sends kittens skittering in all directions. Mama looks up, looks left, looks right, and returns to the business of sustenance.

"I'm going inside," Jason whispers.

"Okay," I whisper back.

He does a decent Elmer Fudd—as in vewy, vewy quiet—on his departure, but Mama Cat acknowledges his movements. She's also aware of me backpedaling to find a more comfortable perch. Patio table and chairs hibernate in the basement, but there's a wash bucket out in the yard; I turn it upside down, a plastic makeshift ottoman. I'm channeling my inner Margaret Mead, Dian Fossey, Osa Johnson. And in a perverse way, I channel (if possible to pervert a perversion) the shy Joe Shmo in the titty bar who doesn't want a lap dance or a special service in the Champagne Room, but simply to have his fancy captured by something at once familiar and foreign. Common yet strange. A concept as much as an entity within his grasp and beyond it. What I'm looking at is a cat, a plain old garden-variety cat, but also a wild thing. The urban bucolic setting—barren trees, fierce evergreen ivy, fallen fences, rubble and earth—adds to this allure. Flaca out in front faced her own daily danger (namely, traffic) but as a creature of asphalt and cement—a stoop cat, the proverbial guttersnipe—she was pedestrian. What I've got here is the genuine article, a bona fide Brooklyn backyard jungle beast. A true feral.

And there's something about the purity of her black and brown stripes—no strain of white infects these markings—that makes her seem exotic. This makes me think of Jenny. Jenny lived on our block when I was a kid—the first crazy cat lady I ever knew, and the first adult outside my family I ever loved. It wasn't strictly felines with Jenny. Woebegone wandered-off dogs; birds with tattered wings; intact, ambitious squirrels all found a way to her back door. But she definitely felt an affinity for cats—stray cats. Independent yet demanding, tough and proud yet exceedingly needful and denying those needs, that was Jenny. She drove a trashed Chevy Impala, drove it like a man, cigarette clinging to the corner of her mouth. Dyed her hair a blatantly brassy blond and cursed a blue streak if you pissed her off. Always in agony (thanks to a shove down a flight of stairs by her father as a child, the survivor of several botched surgeries by her early thirties) but never one to bitch about it. These are things I remember about Jenny, but the thing I remember best is what a clever writer she was.

The only thing she ever wrote, so far as I know, were FREE KITTEN ads to run in the back of the *PennySaver*. Though these ads are rightfully frowned upon by animal rights organizations (not because they devalue a kitten's self-esteem, but because they invite "bunchers"—serious sickos who collect cats and earn filthy lucre selling them to labs), Jenny really had a knack for them. She'd grab one of her latest foundlings by the scruff and, squinting through the smoke of her Kent, assess its qualities in marketing terms—inventing bogus yet believable breeds. A skinny black kitten was a Nigerian Slim, an orange tabby a Mandarin Cheshire, a light-colored cat with dark spots a Portuguese Petit-Point. She created the Icelandic Clipper, which was not a cruise ship line but a large white male with a broken stump of tail, and was about to appoint a timid smoky cat with the title African Grey until she learned there *was* a breed called African Grey—a breed of parrot.

A typical *PennySaver* ad would read:

> FREE KITTENS! *Rare Nigerian Slims! Two male, two female, rescued from flood at top Connecticut breeder, need good homes. Docile, playful, litter-trained. Will go fast!*

What would Jenny have fabricated for the fine-boned, precisely patterned tigress who, having finished a late lunch, now licks a paw with all the delicate poise of Nefertiti's familiar? An Egyptian Sleek? A Nile Valley Velvet?

Whatever she is, her kittens have regained their courage enough to advance on the kibble again. Suffice to say they are so damn cute. Softly I natter inanities in their direction to warm them up to the sound of my voice, which they ignore absolutely, fixated on trying to crunch kibble with milk teeth. Their mother, however, reacts to my rambling, approaching my bucket and rubbing against my legs. Clearly my nonsense is not nonsense at all but enchantment, an incantation; clearly I exude a potent magic that holds wild animals in thrall! Either that, or she, like Flaca, is another ousted house pet, a fully socialized victim of injustice. I can easily assume the source of this injustice. "So what happened?" I gaze down at the cat and cluck. "You get yourself knocked up and they didn't want anything to do with you?"

Sunset is rife with *Homo sapiens* teen moms, but they aren't sent packing. Their apartments get more crowded, a crib by the radiator, a high chair crammed in at the table, a stroller between bikes in the hall. It must be easier to mete out injustice to family members who don't happen to share your genetic makeup. The cat returns my gaze, solid and unblinking. She's a stoic. No shame in her game. It is what it is. She twirls around for another leg rub, maybe not so stoic, maybe fishing for sympathy. She's working it, playing me.

I extend my fingers; she gives a sniff and head-butts my hand. I pet her and she responds with naked appreciation, arching her spine to meet my stroke. I go ear-to-ear, under the chin, right atop the tailbone, scratching, patting, rubbing. I'm running out of tricks here. So I do what I later learn is a major no-no when it comes to feral cats. I pick her up. Fortunately she does not go zombie-stiff with fear, then activate and scratch my eyes out. Instead she purrs with greater intensity and kneads my sweatpants, paw pads leaving mud prints, claws barely scraping the skin of my thighs. The whole time I'm gushing endearments like a member of a pop diva's entourage, telling her how pretty she is, how sweet she is, what a good cat, what a smart cat.

We are having a moment, she and I. A warm and fuzzy moment. The sky is bleak, cold and flat as slate, and I really need a jacket; moreover I really need to be scrubbing the toilet and vacuuming the floors and throwing in another load of dirty clothes and how long have I been out here anyway, interrupting the bliss of banal routine? Outside the day is shortening, darkening, doing those foreboding-type things. Inside the heat is on, music is blasting, chores are waiting. But right here, right now, defying time and space and rock 'n' roll and weather and bathtub ring, a woman and a cat are bonding. If you don't mind. This is where the swell of strings ought to come in.

Except this is when she decides, as cats will abruptly do, that she's had her fill of affection. *Excuse me, let go, down please, thank you.* She lands lightly and stalks a few paces away, just far enough to be out of reach—another thing they do. Then I shiver, and hug myself, and realize we are being watched. The entire PDA, in fact, was duly noted.

The kittens stand in military formation, lined up and staring at us. I figure Mama has been setting a good example. Teaching by doing. Showing her kittens the pleasures of human contact.

"You want some of this?" I lean over on my bucket for a kitten, any kitten will do. I stretch out my hand.

The kittens scatter, furious at the effrontery, then stop and turn to glare at me.

"Oh," I say, reluctantly rising from my perch, which makes them flee farther and duck for cover. "Apparently not . . ."

chapter 3

why can't
we be
friends?

when i lie decrepit, ancient, on my deathbed, and loved ones gather round to beseech some final words of wisdom, I know what those words will be: "Don't . . . ," I will croak, sagacious and, here's hoping, serene, "ever . . . feed . . . stray . . . cats!" Followed, presumably, by: "More . . . morphine!"

The problem with feeding being, of course, feed once, feed forever. Feed once, become the eternal flame of cat food. This is a salient fact I am coming to learn. Cats may have brains the size of a lima bean but they know a good thing when they eat one. Stray? Ha! Whence *that* term? These are not troubadours, gad-abouts, happy-go-lucky hoboes; Woody Guthrie never rode the rails with a feral cat. They're cats, remember—snoozing *is* their job description. Straying requires energy; cats are consummate con-servationists. In this, the urban feline shares a trait with another cosmopolite, the pigeon, who would rather roost than waddle, and will do just about anything to avoid flight—stroll down a bustling Brooklyn sidewalk, and you're practically stepping on tail feathers. Another commonality between cat and pigeon? A built-in homing device: Typically, if a cat happens upon sustenance, he will return—confident, patient—to that same spot awaiting said sustenance to present itself again, like manna from heaven . . . or you.

Sure, the cat will wander minimally from the exact location (for shade in summer, warmth in winter, to police the area for songbirds and squirrels), but about thirty seconds before suppertime he'll reappear with Swiss-watch precision. And lest you forget when suppertime is, he'll remind you by taking up vigil on your windowsill and glaring with an expression universally translatable as: *Oh, you just got home from work? The subway was the third ring of hell? You really have to pee? Fine, go pee—I'll just sit here wasting away in the dark.* When it comes to guilt, Jewish mothers have nothing on feral cats.

So feeding "strays" is a commitment. Trouble is, the average person doesn't think long-term ramifications when confronted by wild animals in the backyard. The average person thinks one of two things: *Where's my crossbow?* or *Awwww!* I, out of touch with my inner Ted Nugent, thought the latter. I fed, initially, on impulse, and now wake every morning and return each eve to find myself at the mercy of feral feline appetites. Fortunately I have my husband's (albeit grudging) approval to serve as meal ticket. Should you ever find yourself in a similar situation, keep in mind that you, too, can gain (albeit grudging) approval from spouse, spousal equivalent, other loved one, roommate, landlord, neighbor, et cetera, if you have noble intentions and the ability to relate them in a positive, rational way. Consider the dialogue between Jason and me two days after the ferals' appearance:

Him: Oh, joy. Look who's here.

Me: Don't worry, sweetie. This is temporary.

Him: Temporary? I don't know. They look pretty . . . settled.

Me: We'll—I'll find homes for them. I promise.

Him: What makes you think you can?

Me: How can I not? Look at them. They're at that irresistible age. Even the mother, she's so sweet; someone will want her. You said yourself someone took Flaca. It won't be a problem.

Him: You think?

Me: Sure!

Logically, then, our next step as foster parents is to name the ferals. The names, like the situation, will be temporary. Placeholders for our convenience. Since we babble about them incessantly (all right, I babble), we can't be referring to them as The Tabby-And-White One, because there are two tabby-and-white ones, so that would be confusing. And The Tabby-And-White One With The Mask is way too cumbersome. And if you're going to name the two tabby-and-white ones, might as well name the others. Because naming animals is fun! And since our time with them will be brief, we might as well make the most of it. Right? Yes!

Actually, Jason sets off the whole naming apparatus. It has come to his attention that when the mother cat approaches—a beckoning hand, a dish of Science Diet—she doesn't beeline directly but comes with a move that bears striking resemblance to the performance style of Guns N' Roses frontman Axl Rose. Not *now*, not Fat Axl, not Plastic Surgery Axl, not the hermetic weirdo who's been making the same comeback album for more than a decade. Lithe, wired, Stephanie Seymour–era Axl. Come on, you remember—that signature serpentine shuffle-weave circa "Sweet Child O' Mine."

"Axl! Here, Axl! Axl Roh-hose!" we singsong amicably to the cat. She does not trot sinuously over. She does not so much as twitch an ear or flick an eyelid in response. Axl it is!

Considering Mama's moniker, it would be simple and efficient to dub her offspring Slash, Duff, Izzy, and . . . the other one, Whatsisname, the one that got fired. Ah, but if we were simple, efficient people we would have opted for the crossbow in the first place. Besides, we are more imaginative than that. We stick to the rock 'n' roll theme yet give the kittens names suited to their personalities.

And what personalities they are. It's only been a few days so I have yet to discern the unique subtleties of each kitten's psychological makeup. Instead I see them as an entity, a unit—a unit worthy of Attila the Hun. Whenever I set foot in the yard the kittens come running toward me, a swarm of hissing, spitting, and snarling. They run with threat low in their throats: *Give us that goddamn kibble before we climb you like a sapling, surgically separate you from your eyeballs, and use them for hockey pucks!*

Ergo the largest of the litter—the tabby-and-white with gangster grillwork—we dub Sid Vicious; his cohort with the matching outfit and heavy kohl eyeliner, Nancy Vicious (fine, forget that self-aggrandizing remark about our imaginative qualities). The half-gray, half-white, half-blind, all-nasty kitten is Ray Snarls. And the runt? What the runt lacks in stature he makes up for in wrath. Of course he's cute—all baby animals are cute, baby rats, baby snakes, they're all cute—but with his beleaguered yet frenzied expression, sporadic sprout of whiskers, and unbalanced markings, let's be real: This will not grow up to be an attractive cat. He looks like a middle school nerd in a hastily homemade superhero costume that earned him the razzing of his classmates. The hissing, snarling, and spitting of Sid, Nancy, and Ray are a choir of seraphim compared with the whacked-out mendacity spewing from this animated beehive in smudgy shoe polish mask and tattered cape. Him we call Paul Wolke. Jason's band, the Vapours, have a song, "Paul Wolke," the lyrics to which were penned by the drummer, Rich, about a shady figure from his past: "What's your game, what is it, Paul Wolke? Are you insane? I really want to know." Paul Wolke immediately gets a nickname: Paulie Walnuts. As in the *Sopranos* character with whom he shares both salt-and-pepper hairstyle and homicidal tendencies.

Yes, all right, I know what you're thinking. You're thinking: *Um, these kittens, these delightful, adorable animals you nobly intend to adopt out—they don't sound very . . . um, nice.* I know you're thinking this because I'm thinking it myself. It's been three days, four maybe, and the rancor has not abated; if anything it has kicked up a notch—the kittens are still sucking the spiritual power that is their mother's milk and on solid food, too; they're getting stronger, tougher . . . *meaner.* I flash on our nation's penal system, basically a farm team for producing stronger, tougher, meaner criminals. I get this vague *ping!*, this internal uh-oh, that maybe I have made a mistake.

I'm concerned, but not too much. Thinking back to my childhood, the teachings of my cat-savior sensei Jenny, I remember crawling under parked cars, dragging kittens out by the scruff, cleaning them up with a squirt of Johnson & Johnson No More Tears shampoo as they clawed desperately for purchase against the porcelain of the bathroom sink and multitudes of astonished fleas eddied down the drain. Once toweled off and blown dry, each kitten (each Flatbush Blue, each Canarsie Seal Point) quickly forgot the indignity and was shuttled off apace to a new home. I look back on all this fondly; it was easy. By next week, I'm sure, I'll have this batch of buggers transformed into snuggly, winning lap-warmers.

But if my distress level is low, two members of the Malkin-Stutts household are on Orange Alert. They have deployed Def Con One. They are freaking out. They are Iggy and Echo, they have become aware of the barbarians at the gate, and they are not happy. Please understand that Iggy and Echo aren't pedigreed show cats; they do not dine on poached salmon in crystal goblets, party on fresh-picked catnip blunts, or win any prize ribbons to honor us with. Echo does not glance out the window and wonder to her brother with amused disdain: "Tell me, dahling, what in heaven's name do you think those wretched creatures might be?" Iggy does not chortle drolly in return, "Really, my dear, I haven't the foggiest notion!"

They know, all right. Iggy and Echo were rescues themselves, shelter cats discovered curled up against each other in a corner of the North Shore Animal League by my mom once one of the kittens Jason and I had already picked out sneezed on me and the vet tech said she had to stay. So no question Iggy and Echo recognize the uncouth usurpers outside for exactly what they are. And think: *There but for the grace of God go we*. Furthermore, Iggy and Echo understand that kibble doesn't grow on trees—and suspect there are limits to the scope and breadth of human affection. True, Jason and I continue to spoil them rotten, but lately I've been spending inordinate amounts of time in the backyard with their rivals, kneeling, cooing, and kibble squandering. Iggy and Echo agree: This is not good.

Iggy and Echo convey their displeasure mostly by leaping from kitchen window to kitchen window with their tails puffed up, smacking the panes with paws of impunity, and emitting guttural warnings that (sorry, guys) wouldn't scare a ladybug. Iggy and Echo may have come into this world as guttersnipes, but a few months in our pampering clutches have turned them into wimps. Iggy especially. Herein lies the risk of naming a cat before his true nature emerges. Iggy screamed hellion-style the entire way from Long Island to Brooklyn, and so was named in homage to Iggy Pop (Echo would repeat his every third howl softly— hence her name). Except Iggy subsequently revealed himself to be a gentle, peaceful, paunchy pansy in formal wear, a cream-filled chocolate chunk, much more Mel Torme's Las Vegas Velvet Fog than Motor City's twisted punk grandpappy. He officially claimed his wimphood when he was small and Jason and I presented him with a life-sized cardboard cutout of a full-grown cat. He thought it was a real cat, puffed up like a demented blowfish, and almost had an aneurysm. We almost died laughing.

Echo has remained a quiet cat—not quiet as in shy white shadow to her brother's barge-like bulk, however; quiet as in stealth bomber. Echo earned the alias Tha Vanilla Killa the first night I ever spent alone in the house (Jason visiting kinfolk down south). I woke to the clumping, batting, squeaking sound of rodent torture, and there was my baby girl, dominatrix in furs. Up the stairs and down the stairs and up the stairs she ran, mouse in mouth, me in pursuit until death (ultimately under the rubber sole of my flip-flop—squishy, crunchy, gross; talk about wimps—I fear I'll never get in touch with my inner Nuge . . .) did they part.

I was duly impressed by Echo's hidden talents. Yet neither she nor Iggy, who should strike fear in the hearts of other cats by virtue of his size alone, get a rise out of oblivious Axl, while her kittens, barely capable of clambering up the sill, stare balefully past the house cats into the house, into my very soul. What's taking me so long with their breakfast? After any stint of kneeling, cooing, and kibble squandering, I return to the kitchen to make amends, but Iggy and Echo are not buying it—they regard me as a traitor, a whore, and stalk off haughtily. Only their favorite treat—one garbanzo bean apiece (accidentally drop a garbanzo bean near a house cat while making your nightly salad, you'll see)—will get me back in their good graces.

A class struggle of haves and have-nots has begun to play out on a daily basis, and I am caught guiltily in the middle. It is time to break out the heavy artillery. Time for Operation Oscar Mayer. Because if you want to have someone eating out of your hand, you'd best get the right bait.

Sunday, a week and one day post-invasion, I embark on my mission, armed with a variety pack of turkey products. Turkey ham, turkey baloney, smoked turkey, honeyed turkey, and, lest there be any purists in the crowd, plain old turkey-turkey. (Truth: The turkey products are not Oscar Mayer. They are not Louis Rich. They are White Rose—New York City's generic supermarket brand of you-name-it, from bleach and aluminum foil to cereal and cold cuts. I may be willing and able to spend a chilly Sunday in December outside on an overturned bucket hoping to socialize a pussycat posse, but I am also cheap.)

Seated on the bucket, I roll a smidgen of meat into a tempting hors d'oeuvre, which I proffer to Axl. She goes for it, enjoying an entire slice of turkey baloney while Sid, Nancy, Paulie, and Ray infringe with utmost caution—unbearably curious, inherently furious. Finally, when Axl has had her fill and steps off, the aroma of compressed turkey parts becomes too much for Ray Snarls. She makes her advance, all twitching nose and malted eyeball, then proceeds to slap the piece of meat out of my grasp, claws extended. Ouch! Yet I do not so much as flinch. "Good girl!" I say as Ray pounces on her prize and gobbles it up off the cement patio.

(This is as opportune a moment as any to mention how I established the kittens' gender. Clearly I did not examine their underparts at this juncture, as I'm not that stupid. I simply decided, by my intuition and their appearance, that Paul and Sidney are male and Nancy and Ray are female.)

I offer another tidbit; Ray accepts with an angry swipe. A left hook, to be precise—maybe we ought to call her Sugar Ray Snarls. She devours, comes back for more, gorging on half a slice before her siblings steel themselves to get in on the action. First pushy little Paul Wolke, then Nancy, lastly Sid—he's proving to be the most aloof of the bunch. I now have all four kittens slapping my digits, a sort of gang-bang ghetto handshake. Soon I know how a pincushion feels. The kittens' insistence on dislodging the meat from me rather than chance any human contact hurts me—physically, emotionally—until I rationalize the pain could be worse if, biting, they failed to discern the difference between processed turkey and the tender flesh of my finger pads.

Around this time my friend Rosemary shows up. With her dark hair, flash smile, milky skin, and eyes like darting minnows, Rosemary is an exotic beauty, a dazzling blend of Irish, Filipino, Caribbean Indian, and I don't know what else. But today, in full clown regalia, she just looks silly. She has driven through Brooklyn on her way to a gig in Staten Island (her husband, Mark, a career clown—no, really—having inveigled her into doing face painting and balloon animals at kiddie parties and corporate functions). Observing me from the back door, she shakes her head with the benevolence of a vastly superior person—and she's wearing three-foot shoes, a fuchsia nose, and voluminous polka-dotted pants. Shamed, I come inside to brew coffee.

"You know," Rosemary says, "you would not believe the crap people can get rid of online." Rosemary is a big Craigslist and eBay enthusiast. "That's where you got to go with these little cats, if you really are trying to get rid of them."

Oh, she thinks she knows me so well! "Of course I'm trying to get rid of them!" I assure her. "I just had no idea. Cats? On Craigslist?"

"Cats, dogs, ferrets, fish," she assures me. "There's definitely heavy traffic in pets."

Now, I may be a conscientious rejecter—a person who eschews many niceties of the twenty-first century, including such technological marvels as cell phones, iPods, Palm Pilots, et cetera— but my friends do not share my Luddite's fear of modern amenities. Rosemary takes out her digital camera and begins shooting the kittens. Several photos come out fuzzy, seeing as Rosemary can't stop giggling every time a kitten gets medieval on my fingers. But some are pretty good—in other words, deceptive enough to depict the savage kittens as sweet, harmless fluff nuggets.

Rosemary e-mails me her efforts that evening (okay, I'm a *selective* conscientious rejecter—I have a computer and an Internet provider), and I enjoy perusing jpgs of the kittens, individually and grouped. But one particular photo gives me pause. It shows not merely a segment of my foot or hand, but all of me—hair busted, attire ditto, not a trace of makeup, lips in a come-hither pucker, surrounded by five cats, only one of whom tolerates my touch. Oddly, I look quite content in this image, but looking at myself looking quite content makes me wince, since I look very much like one of them: a crazy cat lady.

One picture is worth a thousand words? Balderdash! I am *not* a crazy cat lady. I will not endure my friends' yawns of boredom, their eye-rolling insistence that I change the subject. I will not condone my house pets being driven to general anxiety disorder. I cannot permit the continued puncturing of my fingers, which would eventually make typing difficult and interfere with my ability to earn a living. I am divesting myself of these mangy little monsters, posthaste. I frame my Craigslist come-on thusly:

> *Four adorable, playful eight-week-old kittens, plus docile, affectionate mother, need loving home. Take one, take two, or collect all five! References required.*

Talk about false advertising; I might as well be hyping sea monkeys or cellulite cream. True, the copy lacks Jenny's creative flair, but I figure I'm going to hell as it is having left out the part about the hissing, snarling, spitting, and all.

The response is overwhelming. No shit. I wasn't exactly lying when I told Jason "everybody loves kittens!" but I hardly expected discerning Craigslist aficionados to clamor back with demands for more information and additional photography. The last occasion Jason and I had to post on this grab-bag Web site was to offer the top-floor apartment of our brownstone for rent. We knew Sunset Park, being deep in the heart of Brooklyn, lacked the cappuccino-frothed, barroom-infused, boutique- and yoga-studio-bursting appeal of Park Slope or Fort Greene, but we had high ceilings and lots of light and a subway station on the corner. Come on, shelter, that's one of the basic necessities—surely we'd have lots of interest. Instead we had a few clueless inquiries from

New York wannabes who thought the five-room spread for four-teen hundred dollars a month was on 54th Street and Fifth Avenue in Manhattan (which would have placed it squarely inside a Hilton Hotel). The rest of the apartment seekers were multichild families, so we went with what seemed the lesser evil: Lydia and Jessica, two nineteen-year-old art school students who came off bright and cool and responsible.

Uh—not, as we soon found out. These girls do not walk, they stomp—in colossal platform shoes. They do not close doors, they slam them. They do not converse, they scream at each other. They are certainly not bright enough to figure out when the first of the month is, or the color-coded trash can recycling system. Or else they are sociopaths who think rent is optional, and it's Jason's job as landlord to pick through their waste products and redistribute them accordingly. Much of said wrongly placed waste products are beer bottles, so we soon came to refer to our tenants as the Sixpack Sisters. They are textbook examples of what black people mean when they say white children get no home training. And with every stomp and slam and scream that resounds throughout our home (our home!) we pray for summer, when their lease will be up.

So, no, I do not predict this inbox flooded with prospective parents of freaky furbags. And except for the few snobs who want to know the breed of the kittens, whom I summarily ignore (breed indeed!), I feel obliged toward further communication with the people eager to set up appointments to meet them.

"Well," I find myself saying to Sarah and Mike and Evelyn and Gunther and William, "the kittens are . . . well, they're not exactly tame yet."

"Not tame? What do you mean by not tame?" Sarah and Mike and Evelyn and Gunther and William routinely say back.

"Oh, you know, they were born outside, and they haven't really experienced yet the nurturing environment someone like you would provide . . ."

"So that means what?"

Good question. Do you own a pair of falconer's gloves? Have you been the recipient of a tetanus shot during the last ten years? Is there anything in your house or apartment you would mind having smashed, shredded, or otherwise destroyed? What was I thinking, placing this ad? What am I doing taking hours out of my workday to speak to people about cats who could slice and dice them quicker than a late-model Cuisinart?

"Well, I guess it means I need to work with them a little more, get them more accustomed to humans," I say glumly. "But I'll call you in a week if I make progress."

Hmmm. I consider animal shelters, but figure trying to place a cat in one that does not ultimately euthanize will be like trying to get a reservation at Rao's. (I would cite a trendier restaurant, but I don't know any—I have heard, however, about Rao's, the Uptown joint with like five tables you need to be a bona fide goodfella to get into, or perhaps a city councilman or district attorney.) It's not that shelters want to put animals down, but with approximately six to eight million cats and dogs entering shelters each year, according to The Humane Society of the United States, about three to four million are euthanized—there are just so many cages to go around.

My hopes rise when I contact a veterinary clinic in Brooklyn that actually specializes in kitten adoptions, and I'm told they anticipate vacancies shortly. Then my hopes plummet when asked if the kittens are healthy.

I flash on Ray Snarls's marble eye. "Healthy?" I ask.

"Yes," says the receptionist. "Have they tested negative for leukemia and feline HIV? We couldn't take them otherwise—we couldn't risk infecting the other cats."

"Oh . . ." Of course they couldn't. "Do you do testing?"

I am given the days and fees to test kittens for various scourges. But having the kittens tested assumes actually being able to place them in a carrier and take them via car service to the clinic. Hmmm, hadn't thought of that. I make an appointment for the following Wednesday anyway and kick my cat-taming act into high gear.

It is evening. It is quiet. It is cold—winter definitely waking up and kicking in. The ferals have had their dinner and I am administering turkey bribes for dessert. I deliberate. Not Sid—he's got that aura of adolescent thug going on: *Yo, I'm chill, so long as you don't mess with me.* Not Nancy—too skittish and unpredictable. Paul? He's small. But no, he's a mental case. That leaves Ray. Ray seems least disgusted by my presence, was the first to try a piece of turkey infected by my human essence. And, well, she doesn't see so well. She's . . . right . . . there . . . I lean over from my bucket, carefully, silently, holding my breath. All I need to do is snatch her scruff, just like Mama would; her tail will curl under and her back legs fold and she will hang there limply like a moistened paper towel. This is basic to her biology; this is how she will behave.

So I take my shot.

You know how they say bad things happen in slow motion? Well, they're right. Even lightning-fast things. In a matter of seconds that stretch like melting mozzarella Ray goes rigid, then begins to flail and jerk, twist and spasm, every fiber in her seven-ounce soul percolating, paroxysming, electrified, my touch having the shock value of untold volts. I scramble vainly to control her. Her mouth is open but nothing comes out, an Edvard Munch–worthy silent scream. Then with one elasticized contortion, she manages to stab a claw deep into the heel of my palm and hang on as if rappelling a particularly tricky crag of Everest. Oh God, oh God! She's stuck in me, stuck in me good—it takes a couple of shakes to dislodge her. She plunks onto the patio and tears off into the darkness.

In the light of the kitchen I look at my hand. It is enormous. Instantly swollen. A bright red spot of blood where Ray "Captain Hook" Snarls got me. I must be crying as I race upstairs; Jason follows me into the bathroom as I blubber, trying to explain that I am an idiot. Apparently he already knew that. He helps me remove my coat, runs warm water in the sink. Soap, hydrogen peroxide, bacitracin. My hand throbs. My mind wheels. Rabies? Distemper? Oh, God! Oh, Ted Nugent! Cat Scratch Fever? The next morning I make an emergency doctor's appointment for a tetanus shot and prescription for heavy-duty antibiotics.

Alas, no primary care physician can provide the psychological counseling I so clearly require.

chapter 4

hello kitty
creeps
me out

some people sing in the shower. I sing in the backyard. Country ditties. Gospel favorites. Christmas carols. Hits of the 1960s, '70s, and '80s. I am not practicing for my *American Idol* debut; I am crooning to the cats. I want them to know me, know me well—and if they reject me tactilely, I'll come at 'em aurally. How's that for strategy? I talk to them, too, but you know what the bard said about music soothing the savage breast. Besides, any nosy neighbors afoot may consider singing eccentric but soliloquy outright mad.

Not that I need be concerned about pesky Mrs. Kravitz types. Neighbors-wise, we lucked out. On one side there's a semicommercial, semi-residential structure. The commerce part houses a law office specializing in immigration and slip-and-fall accidents, the residential part on the top floor an apartment whose tenants don't have backyard access. On the other side, we have the Hinkleys, who've owned their house since the 1970s. They're liberal-minded, amiable folks who don't mind cats, and best of all they're not around much. Joe Hinkley Sr. has retired to Florida; his son, Joe Jr., is in the process of moving his marketing business and his young family to the Sunshine State as well. The Hinkley abode is occupied by renters, single people with day jobs and night lives and little interest in the possibly eccentric but surely harmless lady next door.

So I sing, opting for lilting, feel-good fare—down-homey material, easy listening, alternapop—since, trust, these cats are aggro enough without the Amphetamine Reptile catalog. Occasionally I sing with Axl on my lap—she's inclined toward power ballads, "Don't stop, beee-lee-vin'/Hold on to that feline, yeah!"—while doling out cuddles to demonstrate the pleasures of person-to-cat contact. She lies her head in the cradle of my palm; she purrs along to the songs; she gazes at me with golden eyes glowing. She is my own personal Paula Abdul.

The kittens, however, are Simon Cowell, cubed.

Everyone at work is aware of my situation—I announce it at the Wednesday production meeting, send e-mails with jpg attachments, post a flyer prominently in the pantry. I am not vying for weird employee of the week—it's just, who knows, maybe someone on staff has been hankering for a kitten. For the most part, however, editorial is either allergic, or has a nice sofa/dog, or is all catted up, thanks. Only one photo editor appears as a potential mark.

"Kittens?" Carla says, *oooh!* implied. She uses a tone you may have heard issuing from the lips of others when they say "cashmere?" or "chocolate?"

"Yes . . . ," I beguile. How easily I have slithered into the salacious role of cat pimp. *"Kittens."*

Carla is in the process of splitting up with her husband; she yearns for a warm body in her bed. She probably hasn't been sleeping well, or she's been sleeping too much—she's got the drowsy-addled-aching look of easy prey. I could have told her I had a covey of fledgling pterodactyls in my backyard and her pupils would've dilated.

But don't think for a minute I intend to foist these kittens on just anybody. I can't be too hasty. There are sickos out there, I know— I watch a ton of *Law & Order Special Vics.* For all I know kitten fighting is the new cockfighting, or kittens are a hot black-market commodity—Karloffian fiends out procuring them for the R&D departments of cosmetics conglomerates. I don't work closely with Carla so must appraise her now with the scrutiny of a prep school dean of admissions. Carla has wide brown eyes and light brown hair in a longish, in-between-styles sort of style; she wears worn-in jeans and neutral colors. Most attractive, she seems gentle and kind, lacking the brittle, neurotic edge of so many media professionals. When Carla softly confesses her imminent divorce, she admits that she feels like she's slipped her moorings a bit—she isn't sure whether this is the best time to take a small, defenseless animal into her life.

"But a kitten, I don't know, maybe two? To keep each other company when I'm not there?" Carla speaks in a wistful voice. "It could be sweet."

Surely this woman's concept of kittens was formed by Disney movies and Hallmark cards and, of course, that ubiquitous branding monolith of the Sanrio Company, Hello Kitty herself. "Well," I tell Carla, "two of the kittens, this brother and sister, they kind of match, and they're soooo cute together."

Shame on me! What am I saying? I can't play down the, shall we say, spit-and-vinegar quotient of Sid and Nancy. "But, you know, you're on the fence, and I don't want to pressure you. Why don't you think about it, and if you feel ready, we can talk more." Then I throw in: "If they're still available . . ."

Well, Carla doesn't mention the kittens again. Fine, I decide, it's for the best; she's probably drowning in a whorl of booze, pills, and self-pity every night, whinily pining for or wilily plotting against her soon-to-be ex—her facade of somber calm around the office precisely that, the veil across the ticking bomb. She could hardly provide a suitable home for these poor kittens. These kittens need stability. They need a steady hand, a steady heart, not some selfish, tormented woman who only wants warm-blooded pillows on which to wipe romantically ruined tears. Or worse. Possibly much worse. Forget it, Carla, you can just forget it—you're not getting anywhere near my kittens, you freak!

Fortunately, while chatting with my deputy editor a few days later, I hear some wonderful news: Fluffy is dead! Granted, this is obviously not wonderful news to Fluffy, or to Fluffy's devoted owner, Maylene, who used to be our copy chief. But for me, news of Fluffy's ascension to a better place is something to seize upon, as Maylene is the ideal candidate for one or four of the kittens. Maylene wants to save the planet. Her office had been cluttered with Greenpeace calendars and PETA paperweights. It was also a veritable clearinghouse of Hello Kitty paraphernalia. In fact the ever-perky Maylene, with her square face and stiff-legged walk, her wide-set eyes and a wardrobe reliant on pastels, is the human embodiment of Hello Kitty. Except, of course, that Maylene has a mouth, and Hello Kitty doesn't, which has always made me find her (Hello Kitty, not Maylene) somewhat creepy.

Anyway, boy, did Maylene ever love that Fluffy! (Note: I have changed some names in this book in order not to piss off some people, but Fluffy really was Fluffy. Maylene, who is not actually named Maylene, considered calling her cat Fluffy ironic.) When Maylene and I were not debating the function of commas around *like* ("he's like totally hot!" versus "he's, like, totally hot!") and other grammatical conundrums of teenage lingo in print form, we were discussing the antics of our house cats. Maylene was prone to joyous rhapsodies when it came to whatever Fluffy did yesterday. Plus, my executive editor confided in me that Maylene resigned to take a job at a magazine that promised saner hours so that she could spend more time with her *cat* (italics are my executive editor's, who confided this to me with an eye-roll stress on the word *cat*). Moreover, Fluffy, if I recall correctly, had been badly abused before Maylene adopted her; Maylene had had to work tirelessly to coax Fluffy out from under the couch. How does one follow up such an accomplishment? By befriending some feral kittens, natch!

I e-mail Maylene to express my sadness at her loss. Then I invite her to lunch. Culling the most benign-looking photos of Axl and company, I head out to meet Maylene in her favorite Midtown Turkish restaurant. I expect the conversation to revolve around Fluffy, and I know to temper my enthusiasm. I can't bulldoze the poor woman with hard-sell schpiel: *Girl, come on, don't live in the past! You've got to move on! And lookee here, I have just the cats for you!* I presume Maylene will be grief-stricken, a basket case, her normally upbeat demeanor dashed. I must act accordingly, tactfully; I can only hint around, show the pictures I just happen to have in my purse, and let nature take its course. If her interest is piqued (and how could it not be?), I'd be more than willing to care for her kitten(s) of choice until she's ready to welcome feline presence back into her life.

So I'm thrown for a loop when Maylene in mourning is as chipper as ever. Her faux leather jacket is adorned with a pussycat pin, the pussycat wearing a jaunty red-and-green holiday bow. Her smile creases her freckles at the sight of me, and she gives me a rather fierce hug for such a petite girl. Dipping pita triangles into baba ghanoush, Maylene fills me in on how her new job actually sucks (started out great, then her boss quit, now she's doing her work and her ex-boss's, and reporting directly to the editor in chief, who's a complete and utter shrew, blah-blah-blah).

"Wow," I say. "Maylene, I'm so sorry. I mean, all that on top of . . . losing Fluffy."

"No, no, no," she says cheerily, this peppermint sprig of a woman. "It's okay. We have found our new cat—Tommy and I are driving up to Buffalo the day after Christmas to fetch her."

Whoa! I think. That was fast. This is not a judgment; Echo and Iggy arrived before Whoopie's cremated remains did. But Buffalo? Maylene and her husband are renting a car and journeying hundreds of miles north in the dead of winter to get a cat, when all she'd have to do is swipe her MetroCard, hop on the N train, and forty minutes, door-to-door, she could have her pick of the litter? Does that sound weird to you? Well . . . wait . . .

"Buffalo?" I am perplexed. "Why Buffalo?"

Maylene is happy to explain. "Well, ever since we lost Fluffy, I've been going to all these pet adoption Web sites. On one level I thought, no, it's too soon—but it was almost as though something, some force, was drawing me there. Oh, Nina, there are so many poor kitties out there! I wanted to take them all. But, you know, our apartment is tiny, so this was a big decision. I had to make sure I chose the *right* cat . . . the one who would be okay with Fluffy."

Far be it from me to condescend to someone's spiritual leanings (you, of course, can feel free . . .) but Maylene has been in contact with Fluffy through a psychic communicator. When Fluffy was alive, Maylene had hired the psychic communicator to translate conversations between herself and her cat, and apparently the psychic communicator is not hindered by the fact that Fluffy is now stone-cold dead. This is one capable psychic communicator! Maylene had tried another one previously who was a real rip-off artist. How it works is, Maylene calls the psychic communicator on the telephone, and the psychic communicator contacts Fluffy (I'm fuzzy on how she does that, exactly). Then, through this metaphysical party line, Maylene and Fluffy can discuss important matters like whether or not it's too soon for a new cat ("It's not!" Fluffy assured Maylene) and which cat would be best. The cat that Fluffy sanctioned is named Mitzvah and is currently residing in a Buffalo feline halfway house.

Am I going to argue with this? I wouldn't know where to begin. I was raised without religion, and no New Agey notions rubbed off during my seven-year residency in Los Angeles. Right now the best I can claim is belief in a Nonspecific Responsible Entity Let's Call Him-Her-It God For Lack Of A Better Term. Who am I to counter this relentlessly perky girl who has a spirit guide give her the hookup to a dead cat? I nod a lot. I eat my stuffed grape leaves and my shish kebab and tell Maylene I hope she and Tommy and Mitzvah will be very happy.

As coffee and dessert are placed on the table, Maylene apologizes for not asking what's new with me. I could tell her about my book deal—my first Young Adult novel out this summer, the second due in six months—or my teen writing workshop, or Jason's band, but instead I tell her about the cats even though she won't be taking one. Because Maylene, as a cat person, might not only slice me some sympathy but is no doubt connected to other cat people, cat people in need, perhaps, of more cats. Plus, let's face it: The cats, like a conversation-eating virus, have pretty much taken precedence over all other topics.

"Kittens?" she says, in that swooning tone—not to taunt me, I'm sure.

"Yeah." I pull out the pictures, but I am glum. "Kittens."

"Oh, they're adorable!"

Yeah, Maylene, tell me something I don't already know.

"What are you going to do with them?"

Please, Maylene, ask me something I can answer. I shrug morosely. "Well, I was hoping to find homes for them—but I . . . now . . . I don't know if that's even possible." A tsunami is building—I think I'm gonna blow. Must be the caffeine-sugar double punch of Turkish coffee and baklava. "Maylene, they're wild. Absolutely run-amok crazy wild. And they loathe me. I go outside with food and water, and they come at me like jacked-up marines storming a beach, like PMS-plagued shoppers at the Barney's Warehouse Sale. I've never seen such vitriol, such unabashed bitchiness—and I've spent twenty years in publishing. And all I want to do is . . . is *help* them. They're so tiny, and it's getting cold, and I thought I could . . . but I can't . . . I'm not . . ."

Maylene clucks. For an instant she seems to want to share my pain. Then she smiles gaily. "Well, you only have one option now," Maylene says. "T! N! R!"

Gimme a T! Gimme an N! Gimme an R! Lunch with Maylene marks my introduction to the three little letters that are to be my obsession over the ensuing months. Maylene fills me in on the process in broad strokes—by now the bill is on the table and she must get back to her sucky job. In addition to Greenpeace and PETA, Maylene supports a New York–based national organization called Neighborhood Cats, the main purpose of which is to educate on, advocate for, and assist in the only viable maintenance solution to the feral feline epidemic: trap-neuter-return. Maylene bubbles about how once you TNR a bunch of cats, they create a vacuum in the territory, their scent a kind of caulk around the perimeter barring invasion by other cats. So, technically, you don't scat any cats. They're yours, lucky you, till death do you part. For ferals enjoying ideal conditions—plenty of food, limited predators, nice weather (Malibu Beach ferals, say), that's about five years max; your basic Brooklyn feral is bound to reach that great scratching post in the sky in a year or two. The point is, with TNR, your established ferals are supposed to keep newcomers away. It's a no-cats-out, no-cats-in deal.

And, of course, no-cats-added. This is crucial. The neuter part is the crux of TNR, the cornerstone. Cats are breeders. The average female can have three litters a year (the gestation period being between sixty-three and sixty-six days), with one to eight kittens per litter. Remember the infamous tribble episode on the original *Star Trek*? The classic film *Gremlins*? That's right, be afraid. It's neuter with vigilance or get a backyard maternity ward. Sure, at two months old our kittens aren't at sexual maturity, but puberty can hit as early as four months, which means Sid and Nancy and Paul and Ray will soon be horny teenagers (queens and toms in cat jargon) with hormones a-ragin'. Not only do I envision them all mounting each other with incestuous glee (oh, stop, this is feline biology, not kitty porn!), there's an even more pressing concern: the fathers of Axl Rose's brood, the kittens' baby daddies.

Yep, plural. Another remarkable feline ability—a queen can mate with a number of toms. Just check the color and markings of the kittens to win at the "Who's Your Daddy?" game. Figuring out who sired Sid and Nancy is a no-brainer when a rangy, tabby-and-white bon vivant with balls the size of kumquats comes bounding out of the bushes. The kittens scram, billiard balls in a break. Axl gives him that icy *Do I know you? Mmm, no, excuse me, I don't think I do* look and proceeds to wash her face conscientiously. The big cat couldn't care less—he saunters straight up to me, a *Hidy-ho, neighbor!* meow out of his mouth, his tail sticking up like the antenna of a muscle car. After a forward-back-forward mambo between my shins, he arches, looks up at me, and demands to be petted.

I acquiesce, first with a quick scritch to the coccyx, then a rub between the ears. That's when I notice a furrow in the fur around his neck, a rut that could only be caused by . . . holy tabby-and-white collar crime! Another perfectly good cat that some asshole got bored with and abandoned. Or possibly he's not a full-on orphan—he doesn't show much interest in the kibble I've catered, so he's probably still getting fed elsewhere. Maybe he grew up and started spraying willy-nilly, which led someone to pronounce him "outdoor only." Some guy, no doubt—sorry to get all sexist but you know how funny guys are about testicles and this cat was cast out in full possession of his *cojones.*

Of course this is pure conjecture. I'm just assuming. My other, stronger, assumption is that this tomcat's gene pool is persevering in Nancy and Sid, who are patterned after him. And while Axl may be able to ignore the dude now, the second she goes into heat again—every fourteen to twenty-one days!—she'll be come hither howling for him.

Or . . . the other one. He shows up a day later. Friendly? Hard to tell. At first I'm not even sure he's not vegetable or mineral. Getting ready for work, I glance out the bedroom window to bear witness as a solid black rock or a clump of dirt stands up, stretches, makes a tight circle, and sits back down again. Baby Daddy #2—his DNA on display in Paul Wolke and Ray Snarls—is just biding his time.

Back at the office I promptly go online to investigate further. Go ahead, plug "trap neuter return" into your favorite search engine—it is edifying. Cyberspace teems with reams on why TNR works, and why other alternatives do not, plus how-to guidelines and helpful tips for the "caretaker" (um, I suppose that would be me) of the "colony" (aka assorted nasty furbags). Colony, huh? Conjures an image of pre-Revolutionary America: Plymouth Rock and tobacco fields and no taxation without representation. And slaves, of course—the colonies were built on chained labor. Then I think sci fi: the colonization of some barren, multimooned planet. Finally I think ants encased in glass. "Colony" feels momentous and mysterious and vaguely icky to me.

Assuming my employer factors in only a certain amount of Web loafing into the equation that determines my salary, I don't spend the rest of the afternoon online. Instead, I print out selections of TNR literature for further study, and as I rumble across the river to Brooklyn that evening, I reread several times the passage about how withdrawing food will not make cats disperse. It will make cats scrawny, it will make cats irritable, and it will make you feel like reprehensible scum, but it will not make cats take off in search of meatier pastures. There is a sense of entitlement to cats—if you casually toss a chicken bone in their direction, they will fully anticipate that the chicken bones will keep coming, with regularity, none of this dilly-dallying. It is a feline law of physics: A source of food will reoccur if you glare at the spot where it first appeared long enough. (This is not to recommend tossing a chicken bone at a cat; quite the contrary. In his attempt to devour the entire chicken bone, the cat could easily wind up with a shard in his gullet and choke to death. If you are going to toss something at a cat, might I suggest a nice filet mignon?)

I know for damn sure watching catsicles form outside my kitchen window would drive me out of my mind with guilt. And speaking of madness, it dawns on me that the cool part about TNRing our backyard squatters is, it would allow me to keep them. Why this is appealing, I cannot fathom. The more I bow and scrape, the more the kittens revile me. Were it not for the twice-daily rations I dole out they'd have nothing whatsoever to do with me. Not that they'd prefer their plates to be miraculously refilled without me. They seem to get some pleasure from racing toward me, hissing and spitting and so forth, like a hockey team from hell—it's like a workout for their malice muscles. So wanting them around, courting their constant fury, doesn't make a whole lot of sense. Staying with a moochy boyfriend makes more sense, working in an industry funded by Satan makes more sense, smoking cigarettes makes more sense (not to say I have ever actually practiced any of the aforementioned). Submitting to the animosity of these animals is pure masochism, without the shiny hardware or orgasmic payoff (not that I've actually practiced that, either).

But even if I'm willing to throw sanity to the wind, what about Jason? He may not be above the occasional televised bout of professional wrestling, he may believe the work of the Dead Milkmen to be high art, but he is at his core a logical individual, a fact-checker, in fact, by trade. And a southern man. Forget all that yes ma'am gentility they spout; there is nothing more stubborn than a southern man. Crackers, all right—crackers made of stone, crackers you can break a tooth on. How am I to convince him lawn ornaments that piss and poop are eminently more desirable outdoor decor than run-of-the-mill garden gnomes or (more prevalent in Sunset) turn-of-the-century plumbing fixtures (a claw-foot tub or pedestal sink filled with shrubbery is de rigueur around here)?

I could appeal to his squishy side—present the ferals as a misbegotten family. Make it sound all Dickensian—*Christmas Carol* or *Oliver Twist* or somesuch—throw in a musical number with kittens in threadbare stockings and secondhand stovepipe hats dancing a merry jig. Quickly, I strike the idea. Jason's in no mood—he couldn't get enough days off to make a trip to South Carolina for the holidays this year. He's missing his human family, so trying to pass off the furbags as a replacement for blood kin probably won't win me or the furbags any favor.

So I break out the documents. Hard cold hard copies detailing the validity of TNR. I put it to him thusly: Plan A is still in effect—I will continue acclimatizing the kittens to human beings until I am able to parcel them out. But now we have a Plan B. A contingency measure. Trap! Neuter! Return!

chapter 5

gimme
shelter

epiphany hits on the bucket.

Sitting there in cat-tamer attire (puffy coat, pajama bottoms, Doc Martens, earmuffs . . . geez, the ultimate fashion sin: *earmuffs*), I watch the wind stir naked limbs of maple, mimosa, the borough's signature Brooklyn trees. A ragtag bunch of ravers, hands in the air and grooving like they just don't care. Give the branches glo-stix and smart drinks and the visual is complete. The image makes me smile and, smiling, I realize I've been taking this cat thing way too seriously. I've mythologized the kittens, made them into Minotaurs, Medusas, creatures you'd see in an old *Sinbad* flick or something starring The Rock. But come now, they're just kittens, right? And what do kittens like to do? Kittens like to play!

So as the furbags finish their AM repast, I surreptitiously step around them to find a nice long stick (*Ren & Stimpy* aficionados will recognize this as Log, Jr.). Then I return to the bucket and settle down to tap and scratch cement. Someone alert the Neptunes—Chad and Pharell are going to want to get this on tape.

What's that noise? Oh, that's a cool noise, a fascinating noise. We must find the cause of that noise—and kill it!

That's me thinking like a kitten. Because the kittens do respond. Mostly, they respond as though my having the temerity to attempt engaging them in play is a ludicrous, potentially injurious caper. Sidney offers his enigmatic stare, Nancy seems daft but bored, and Paulie, as usual, looks enraged. Ray Snarls, however, is intrigued. Not that she *does* anything, or anything the naked eye could observe. But inside Ray Snarls, pistons are firing—she is tensing, prepping, poising, plotting. If you live with a cat you're acquainted with this stance. It feels as though a complete Stephen King miniseries could ensue, a species could evolve, in the pre-pounce period: You dangle a toy and wait, wait, wait for frozen cat to thaw.

Finally, Ray does. Takes a step . . . lifts a paw . . . swats the stick. Yes! Yay! She swats it!

I drag, she follows; I tap, she bats—left paw, right paw, left; lemme at that damn stick, I'm gonna murderlize that stick, that stick is mine, mofo, that stick is dead meat. "Good girl!" Cold air shows my breathless whispers in puffs. "Get the stick! Get it, get it! Oh, you're so smart! Oh, you're so fierce. Oh, you're just the best kitten ever!"

We are playing, me and Ray Snarls, together, playing stick. Now, where's that Nobel?

I neglect my agenda. Second novel with looming deadline? Haven't written word one. And even though it's the holiday season, when the media industry merrily goes brain dead, work is nuts: We're closing an issue while my boss attempts to reinvent the wheel, crashing a last-minute story, adding a new front-of-book section, tediously tweaking the coverlines (Get *Hot* Hair Now! versus Get Hot

Hair *Now!*). Yet here I am, thoroughly preoccupied by the gang of miscreants in the primeval hinterlands behind our house.

What I don't understand is *why*. Emotionally, this is turning out to be far more than I bargained for, yet out I trot, morning and night, a sartorial atrocity, tempting with treats, seducing with sticks. I'm the chick who hates a challenge, remember. I certainly never applied myself with this kind of diligence toward advancing my career—when other upwardly mobile professionals were networking, ass-kissing, and backstabbing I was . . . well, I don't remember but I'd wager ice cream or vodka was involved. So why the hell am I working so hard?

Perhaps it's karma for having pooh-poohed my biological clock, to the point that I failed to even wind it. Having babies, raising kids, never entered my consciousness—I didn't play with dolls, never fantasized about motherhood while doodling some high school crush's name in a heart on a looseleaf binder. I'm not one to coo over infants. My personal hell would be a baby shower. Not that I dislike children. Children are people—some I like, others not so much—but I feel no compulsion to spring any off of my own. To be blunt, I'm too darn selfish (and fortunate to have married a man who's big on birth control). So maybe this blight of kittens is payback for deviant nonmaternal instincts. Of course, some would say I'm in denial—now that I'm slouching toward menopause I regret not reproducing, and project this thwarted need on the furbags. But nah.

A more likely explanation would be sibling rivalry. My elder and only sister Donna, who goes by Ginger, is in the process of a very colorful life, which has included, between careers as a go-go bar bartender and a Christian missionary, a stint as a semi-professional lion tamer. She pursued this field while residing in the great state of Nevada. You know how fast and loose they are about guns and hookers out there? Well, you can get an exotic animal permit pretty easily, too, and in addition to parrots, birds of prey, and a small pack of demented wolves Donna amassed lions, tigers, and cougars (oh my!) that she attempted to train in the hope of landing a gig at one of the Vegas theme hotels.

The closest she got was an eagle-and-falcon act at an arena-seating dinner theater where wenches feed you Cornish game hen without benefit of knives or forks and knights on horseback joust for your further enjoyment. Things didn't work out over the long haul and a lot of animals got sick and died so Donna ultimately abandoned the project to save the souls of a small African village. Following a nasty bout with a rare form of cancer, she returned stateside to attend surgical assistant school in Virginia, where her landlady does not allow pets, not even goldfish.

Still, though the woman has trained five-hundred-pound tigers and I can't even handle an eight-ounce pussycat, the sibling rivalry explanation doesn't sit right with me, either. Not to be judgmental . . . but what the hell: I don't really approve of the keeping of exotic animals. (Not that my disapproval prevented me from once experiencing the joy of romping with my sister's two-month-old tiger cub back in the day.) Besides, Donna doesn't live in Brooklyn; it's not like she's waltzing into my backyard with a smirk on her face and a wild beast draped casually across her shoulders.

So what gives? Why am I the one jumping through hoops?

The answer flattens me like an anvil. Embarrasses me, too. Really, I thought I was all done with that crap.

Check it out: With Jason I have built a solid relationship with a do-the-right-thing, all-around-wonderful human being. We have health insurance. We have a mortgage. We have a *marriage*. While we may appear an odd couple from the outside (our age and cultural discrepancies; his staunch preference for Beck's *Mellow Gold*, mine for *Odelay*), our lives are a model of comfortable, staid domesticity. And I like it fine. I *love* it fine.

However . . .

The allure of these cats comes down to one thing for me. Savagery. Ostensibly I'm seeking to subdue them, but I want to be around them precisely because they are wild. This, I am loath to admit, is nothing new. All through my extended adolescence I dated boys least likely to meet with parental approval. The skinny loner/loser in the leather jacket with the reliable drug connect and the Ramones tapes. Probably a bass player. Indubitably a band boy. Aka a bad boy. Antisocial? Unemployed? Bipolar? Prinking droblem? Come to Mama! A condition commonly known as Irritable Boy Syndrome (IBS). I thought Jason was the antidote, and in matters of romance he is—my band boy with the heart of gold and the moral fiber of titanium. Except the symptoms of what enslaves me now feel all too familiar.

And whoa! When I give my condition further unflinching study, the mind reels. This is not merely a feline manifestation of IBS—*au contraire*! What afflicts me now, I recognize, is the essential, original malady. Before puberty, back when boys—all boys, good, bad, whatever—were yucky, when sex, drugs, and rock 'n' roll were not remotely on the menu, I was crawling under cars for cats. *Wild* cats. I have come full circle. I suffer anew from a chronic ailment that has been in remission. Wild Cat Syndrome.

Though I've been taking liberties using it as a noun, *Merriam Webster* defines *feral,* an adjective, as

1: of, relating to, or suggestive of a wild beast; 2a: not domesticated or cultivated; b: having escaped from domestication and become wild.

It's b that gets me, the whole escaping-domestication idea, which suggests a conscious dismissal of the orderly, the aligned, the comfy-cozy. Okay, I don't really believe that—I know animals with brains the size of a lima bean didn't hold a quorum and decide on a back-to-nature policy à la 1970s flower children. Ferals go feral, as I've naggily noted on these pages and will no doubt find cause to naggily note again, thanks to the very species that domesticated them, whose brains are approximately the size of grapefruit.

I simply like to pretend that cats are born to be wild, that wild is their preference, and while I'd be a broken woman if Iggy and Echo ran away from home in pursuit of feral freedom, that wildness is what I marvel at and admire most in the kittens. The state of our yard factors into it, too. Sure, part of me yearns for a garden Martha Stewart would covet and a patio composed not of cracked cement and the found bricks my husband pushed into the dirt, but of neat paving stones. Yet this lost world of weeds and ivy, ramshackle fences, and enough dangerously droopy power lines (viperous telephone cables, electric cables, cable cables) to make R. Crumb drool, is the badass bucolic backdrop to our feral melodrama. Happy homemaker I may be, but on some level noble savagery has stubborn appeal.

Since I'm copping to my shit, let's take it to its logical conclusion. Watching the tragic documentary *Grizzly Man*, about self-appointed bear conservationist and certifiable head case Timothy Treadwell, a shiver of simpatico runs through me. I repeatedly interrupt Jason's enjoyment of the film to insist, "That's *not* me! I am *not* like that!" Yeah, well. Methinks the lady doth protest a tad. It's petty, it's selfish, it's immature, but I get where Treadwell is aching from. I wanna be Max in Maurice Sendak's *Where the Wild Things Are*—crowned king of beasts.

I pour my cat-possessed soul out to longtime friend Gini. True, I'll pour my cat-possessed soul out to anyone who'll half listen, but I figure Gini and her husband, Dave, will be especially compassionate, as they are the kind of people cats walk all over. To wit, Earwig, one of their three indoor–outdoor foundlings, has a tendency to leap onto the dining room table, eat a morsel off Dave's dish, then waltz over to Gini's plate and upchuck it there.

Over the years these kind, decent, exceedingly foolish people have taken in and adopted out many a cat, not to mention the cats who for one reason or another veterinarians recommended they, at their own expense, euthanize (which led Gini to dub herself "the Kevorkian of cats"). Recently Gini and Dave's cat situation stabilized; they are a far less active feline underground railroad since macho El Mysterioso, another of their foundlings, began to bully all trespassing *gatos* off the grounds. Plus, while Gini loves her cats, she has taken up with ducks lately (she has two), and compared with cats, waterfowl are pretty exotic.

The episode of our saga I choose to share with Gini, in a fairly hysterical, gasping flume, concerns my discovery that cats follow strict rules of predictable behavior only to break them in order to freak you out. For the past twenty-four hours or so I have been kitten-free—and I dial Gini frantically to impart my theory as to why.

"There's this baby daddy who comes around [gasp!], and he—I'm convinced—he's killed the kittens [gasp!]. Do they do that? Do they eat their young? I've heard that they do that. [Gasp!] Why would he do that? I haven't seen the kittens in a whole day—[gasp!]—the mother is around but the kittens are gone, and what else could have happened? Where could they be? [Gasp!] Jason doesn't believe me, he thinks I'm nuts, but come on, it's obvious. You should see his nose—it's all scratched up. Clearly this . . . [gasp!] this monster has murdered his own children!"

Gini does her best to soothe me, but I don't want to be soothed. I want validation of the possibility that Baby Daddy #1 (whom I've been calling Bobby Darin but may need to rename Marvin Senior) has committed infanticide. When she gives it up, I tell Jason, my voice a self-righteous tremolo: "Gini thinks it could happen!" The next day, when the kittens come toddling back, la-di-da like they'd caught the Chinatown bus to the Mohegan Sun casino for the weekend, I submit to Jason's teasing, then call Gini to sheepishly report all is well.

"You might want to talk to Sheri and Sean about all this; they've got wild cats in their yard." Gini directs me to friends of hers, since all the cats she's ushered in and out had been social, not savage. "Better yet, talk to Matt and Amy. I'm not sure of the details but I think Amy was connected to some kind of wild cat society for a while."

The idea of forming a feral support group appeals to me, but I cannot bring myself to reach out to Sheri and Sean. Frankly, I find Sheri and Sean rather intimidating. Although Sheri and Sean have never been anything but lovely on the occasions I've met them, her fiction has been glowingly compared to Dickens *and* Proust in the *New York Times Book Review*, and I think he has four, maybe six PhDs in fields I can't even pronounce. I quite sensibly surmise that *their* ferals don't swarm, hissing and spitting, at the sight of them. Surely *their* ferals take snacks from their hands without benefit of a claws-bared slap. In fact, *their* ferals must have obligingly volunteered to be TNR'd, and were you to stroll into Sheri and Sean's backyard you'd see a bevy of intelligent, talented, well-mannered cats playing croquet and besting one another at anagrams.

Not that Matt and Amy are troglodytes or anything. They must be real smart—they're also friends with Sheri and Sean—I just have no specific reason to be cowed by them and have actually been meaning to get in touch since discovering, at one of Gini and Dave's parties, that Matt and Amy are Sunset homeowners, too. We'd gabbed about the joys and sorrows of the hood, Amy and I bonding big-time over the lack of quality produce and virtually anything low-fat.

We meet up at the Mexican restaurant of their choice. Amy's maybe five feet tall stretching; Matt's about six-five slouching. She's got deep brown eyes and a sleek bob that resembles the petals of a hothouse tulip; he's fair, shaven of pate, and recalls a stalk of wheat. She's in fund-raising; he's in IT. Each came to the relationship with three house cats, and each had a feral plight.

When Matt purchased his house on the northern rim of Sunset (Jason and I are a mile or so south, near the border of Bay Ridge), he didn't know it had the added bonus of beasties: a litter of kittens delivered in an adjacent commercial structure. Philosophizing that it could have been termites—which are ostensibly more destructive and, well, less cute than kittens—he became a hapless yet intrepid trapper. "Matt's method was to just grab a cat and throw it in a carrier," Amy says indulgently as Matt shows off his scars. He'd sequester his quarry in a separate room—away from his house cats, so they'd be none the wiser—then set about teaching the social graces. Two kittens were won over and adopted out. (They later died of feline immunodeficiency virus, commonly known as feline AIDS, which is reported to affect between 1 and 8 percent of apparently healthy cats in the United States. Similar to human AIDS, but not transmittable to people, it is present in the saliva of infected cats and transmitted through bite wounds.) Matt's other two ferals would have none of this fraternizing *bool*-shit, so Matt proceeded with neuter and return—and continual valet duties.

Though Amy lived in Manhattan at the time, she was becoming a feral paraprofessional, thanks to her friend and coworker Ellen, a resident of Ditmas Park. One of Brooklyn's showplace neighborhoods, Ditmas Park, aka "historic Flatbush," is known for beautiful, rambling Victorian houses, lush-boughed trees, and an anachronistic small-town aura (in other words, it ain't no Sunset). It's the kind of place where trendily dressed children of many hues play outside in safety and harmony. It's so quaint, in fact, that a local theater company recently staged a production of *To Kill a Mockingbird* on its ample wide porches. That said, Ditmas Park is not paradise. It being part of a free country, assholes are allowed. A family of such assholes lived across the street from Amy's friend Ellen. These particular assholes were cat fanciers with ADD: Every six to ten months or so they would acquire a new kitten, and when they got bored with it would show it the door—and replace it with another new kitten.

Ellen started feeding the orphans on her porch. Dumb move, Ellen. Kind move, sweet move, but dumb as dirt. Before long Ellen and her husband were running a kibble soup kitchen while learning the trials and errors of TNR. Naturally, this became Ellen's primary topic of conversation around the watercooler ("Did you see *Desperate Housewives* last night?" "Who gives a damn—those lunatics across the street dumped another cat!"). As it turned out several women in the office also had "a situation," or were simply so appalled by Ellen's they wanted to help. Since they were in fund-raising, they got all Judy Garland–Mickey Rooney about it: "Let's start a nonprofit!" For Paws was born.

"We kept our full-time jobs, and would work on For Paws till midnight, but it was fun," Amy says. "We had events to raise money—a foosball tournament, swing dance night." In time, For Paws was ready for its first "spay day." Who knew the ASPCA has a "you tricks 'em, we fix 'em" policy? Nab a phalanx of felines, they will send a mobile surgical unit to your doorstep. For several days, For Paw-ers baited and waited, snagging some twenty-three cats in toto. A resounding success—among the cats spayed were six adult females, each pregnant with five fetuses about to be expelled into an unkind world. "It was satisfying," Amy says. "But there's nothing warm and fuzzy about aborting thirty kittens."

For Paws continued to do more mass trappings and educational outreach, but when the founders tried to grow the organization—take it beyond Brooklyn, affiliate with other groups—bureaucracy, as well as humanity (Ellen became pregnant, another member moved out of state), led For Paws to go to the dogs.

Listening to Matt and Amy, I know we have definitely come to the right couple. In addition to the illuminating horror stories, they provide practical info—about, for instance, Muffin's Pet Connection, an animal aid organization that, among other things, offers discount spay/neuter certificates redeemable at participating vets in New York City (go to muffins.org for more info). When Matt asks what kind of shelter we have for our ferals, I'm proud to tell him we've got that covered: "I took an old down coat and stuffed it into a garbage can," I say. "They hang out in there."

Matt and Amy exchange a glance.

"What?" I ask. "No good?"

"Well, it hasn't rained recently . . . ," says Matt.

"It hasn't snowed yet . . . ," says Amy.

"It hasn't really been that cold . . ."

Will they please stop pussyfooting around!

"We don't want to tell you guys what to do . . ."

"But you really should build them a shelter . . ."

"Something waterproof . . ."

"And insulated . . ."

"Build?" Jason glances up from his burrito. The very word brings out the Bob Vila in my man. Matt and Amy describe a sturdy structure that can keep several full-grown cats—or Axl and her offspring—warm and dry all winter, and can be easily, economically assembled from materials available at any lumber and hardware establishment.

I insist on picking up the check.

The next day I print out the cat house blueprints from the Neighborhood Cats Web site (this TNR advocacy and educational agency is a wonderful resource; go to neighborhoodcats.org). But when I show them to Jason I encounter unexpected resistance. Jason, it seems, has been "thinking."

And Jason doesn't keep his thoughts to himself: "I think I can dig them a shelter in the dirt mound—sort of like an igloo."

He's been itching to make use of that damn mound of dirt, aka Mount Stutts, aka J2. It was formed last spring when Jason, seeking to level the area closest to the house so as to extend the patio, dug up the yard, flinging extraneous dirt toward the nether reaches. (Tangent alert! During the excavation, Jason went amateur archaeologist, unearthing a Mason jar filled with red fluid, a faded photograph, hair, and a pair of ladies' panties—possibly a thong. We were not shocked by The Jar—that Santeria and Voodoo would be practiced in Sunset was no surprise—but what to do with The Jar was a big issue for about a week. One *consigliore* insisted we bury it back in the yard, another said to throw it in the trash; eventually we contacted the Seventy-second Precinct and entrusted The Jar to the bemused uniforms who answered the call.)

"An igloo?" I respond.

Unfortunately "that tone" has infiltrated my voice. I hate "that tone" almost as much as the person on the receiving end hates it, who eight times out of ten is someone I love (one time out of ten it is a civil servant and the other time it's a telemarketer). "That tone" is a stress response, a defense mechanism—it rears its ugly sound when I feel threatened—in this case, when I feel threatened that I'm not going to get my way. It would be one thing if "that tone" hypnotized my opponent and made him do my bidding. But "that tone" is pretty damn useless—if anything it makes my opponent more opposed to me. Would that I could control "that tone"; alas it comes without warning—just parks itself in my sentences in all its shining bitchy glory. A therapist might call this a lot of malarkey, and say there are steps I can take to keep "that tone" at bay, but somehow I've managed to attain middle age without finding time or budget for such luxury as therapy. So I continue, "that tone" intact: "You want to dig the cats a dirt igloo."

Yeah, yeah, yeah, Jason loves me unconditionally but he doesn't let me get away with a goddamn thing.

Ding! Round one!

Jason, employing a tone of his own, begins to explain the fundaments of igloo architecture. I don't want to hear them. Why should my already hardworking husband court muscle spasms, plying stony winter dirt, on an unprecedented igloo experiment when I have perfectly good plans for a tried-and-true shelter right here? How did his enthusiasm to lock and load his table saw get usurped by this desire to shovel?

I flash on how my boss, who is an amazing manager, a true force of nurture, would have reacted if someone came up with the editorial equivalent of a dirt igloo in a pitch meeting. "Wow, a dirt igloo!" she would no doubt say. "I love that kind of creative thinking! I'm not sure that it's the best way to go right now, but it's such a novel concept, will you send me a memo on it and re-mind me about it in the future? You rock!"

Yeah, well, there's a reason she's an editor in chief and I hit my glass ceiling a decade ago.

"But look." I extend the blueprint. "See? This is what the experts say to do, and this is what *I* want us to do." What I want is this igloo nonsense to go away, but the more I disdain it, the more Jason counters (have I mentioned he can be as obdurate as a heavy-metal riff?). The argument continues for about a day and a half, and the only reason he gives in is because "that tone" wears out and the tears come on. Yes, I weep. Yes, I fight dirty.

Jason and I head to our local Home Depot to obtain the nec-essary materials. The trouble is, because we own no motor vehi-cle, a trip to our local Home Depot is akin to a trek across the tundra. Those are some loooong, desolate blocks from the sub-way station to the Home Depot, especially in the rain. But we do it—we do it together! An adventure! A project! Life's a frolic!

Estimated retail price of cat shelter materials? Twenty-five dollars. Somehow, a hundred bucks later, Jason and I struggle to get two eight-foot slabs of Pink Panther–pink Styrofoam through a subway turnstile (only one eight-foot slab of Styrofoam is required, but we buy two just in case we mess up). Once home, Jason lays out plans, materials (caulk, linoleum tile with adhesive backing, and latex deck paint), and tools (table saw, utility knife, caulk gun, paint roller and tray, yardstick, and felt-tip marker) in the basement. He starts getting psyched again about the project. Plus, he has me at his side, his eager, able-bodied assistant. Not as able-bodied as Pamela Anderson as the Tool Time girl on *Home Improvement*, nor as scantily tricked out, but Jason's still glad to see me braving the basement. I am afraid of the basement. It's clammy. The floor is dirt and the ceiling is all wires and girders and cobwebs. The basement also lodges the boiler, and I am afraid of the boiler as well. I refer to the basement as the dungeon and except for the lack of a rack and wall-mounted manacles it's not so far off.

We set to work and within several hours have an eighteen- by twenty- by twelve-inch shelter. It looks just like the drawing! I run Sunday's Arts & Leisure section through the paper shredder—that de rigueur appliance necessary for all those paranoid about identity theft—to make a plush pile carpet for the interior. I can barely wait for the paint and caulk to dry. I'm so proud of us—I just hope the cats will feel the same.

chapter 6

trick,
neuter,
return

new year's eve is no whoop-de-do holiday for me. Okay, maybe when I was little and got to bang on pots and pans. Nothing beats a good pots-and-pans bang, but I can have one on any given Tuesday in April, and I don't have to ask permission. A perk of adulthood. A downside of adulthood is the unceasing march of time, so why celebrate it? What a waste of party dress. Might as well call it Neuralgia's Eve, Alzheimer's Eve. Resolutions? Surely you jest. I make but one concession to New Year's Eve, and that is to polish off an entire bottle of decent champagne. Solo. Jason hasn't touched alcohol since the time he tried to drunkenly dissuade a mugger and received for his efforts twelve stitches in the head. (An incident that occurred, by the way, not in Sunset Park but in Kips Bay, my erstwhile Manhattan neighborhood—an East Side hot spot per realtors citywide.) Anyway, if I start around eight thirty I will near the bottom of the bubbly by midnight, and only by setting this goal can I manage to stay up that late.

This New Year's, however, Jason and I hope to have something solid to commemorate: our triumphant entry into TNR.

Although the *T* is erroneous. More like *D*, for deceive, or *C*, for con. We have initiated Operation Cat Nap, an exercise of such subterfuge and bamboozlement, the current administration would be proud. A Muffin's Spay/Neuter Certificate has been pre-ordered and arrives in the mail, but upon absorbing the ramifications of this slip of paper my courage and commitment waver. I need affirmation, guidance. A pep talk. I dial the agency's phone number and confide in a woman named Jude.

"I really don't know what I'm doing," I say, "and I feel, I don't know, the whole thing is kind of sneaky."

Jude has evidently heard this before. "You're doing the right thing," she intones in a voice like superfine steel wool. "You'll be fine. The cat will be fine." When Jude starts getting religious on me, telling me that I'm doing God's work, I become confused. How can TNR be God's work, Him being the one to coin the phrase "be fruitful and multiply"? And what if Axl is pregnant? As far as I can tell she's been conducting herself as a proper lady, but might she not have slid into heat while I was at work and got pounced by Bobby Darin or Homer Joy? (Homer Joy, that's Baby Daddy #2, named for the guy who wrote "The Streets of Bakersfield" and in particular the line "You don't know me but you don't like me," clearly this cat's attitude toward yours truly.) Personally I am pro-choice. I haven't discussed gender politics with Axl. I am making the choice for her. If you're going to be domineering you might as well get some pleasure out of it—but as Amy said there is nothing warm and fuzzy about aborting kittens.

I thank Jude and hang up.

On the day before New Year's Eve, I call a vet on the Muffin's list to make an appointment. Next, I borrow a hard-case pet carrier from Gini and Dave. When Iggy and Echo take an excursion, they have a nylon, fleece-lined gym-bag sort of thing, which I fear will never do. Having no idea how Axl will react to betting snatched, I'm thinking a more rugged conveyance might be in order.

Then I starve the cats. Spaying is major surgery, so no food or water for Axl the night before; plus I want to make sure she's extra docile and friendly—i.e., weak—when I hit the yard in the morning.

The kittens come bounding out of their new domicile, greeting me in their usual manner—flume of hatred in four-part harmony—but I ignore them, focusing on Axl instead. Can't get too comfortable since I'll need to be fleet, so I squat above the bucket, and as the unsuspecting Axl rubs against my shin I give her a few insincere strokes before scooping her up and rising to my feet in one less-than-fluid motion. In three strides I'm at the back door, which Jason holds for me; then it's into the bathroom.

Our abductee remains calm and pliant in my fiendish clutches; if she's aware of being inside she's not too worried. The carrier sits open on the toilet seat, and only when Axl gets a glimpse or whiff of the contraption, or maybe a precognitive flash on its purpose, does she start to comprehend that a caper is afoot. She begins to wriggle as I drop to my knees before the throne, pressing my torso toward the carrier. The only options Axl has are forward, into the carrier, or up—climb me like a telephone pole. Fortunately for me she does not ascend. An avocado pit of guilt lodges in my throat, but at least I have not had my face ripped to pieces.

I shut the carrier and latch it. Axl begins to moan—low, loud, pitiful. I blush with blame. Jason calls Mexicana, the car service we like. A maroon Lincoln virtually astral-projects; it is honking in front of our house before I can act on my second, third, nine-teenth thoughts and spring Axl from lockdown. Jason arranges the carrier on my lap and I tell the driver the address. We're off!

"Shh, shh!" I whisper to Axl, who ululates anew. "It will be all right, I promise."

The driver heads for the Brooklyn-Queens Expressway.

"Jason, where is he going?" I want to know, sibilant, nervous. "Is he getting on the BQE? Why is he getting on the BQE?"

We like Mexicana Car Service because the drivers are always mellow. They don't, however, speak a lot of English.

"Hey, man," Jason says. "You getting on the BQE?"

"Heh?" queries the driver.

"The BQE? You're getting on the BQE?"

"Ai, *sí.* BQE!"

"No, no! Why?" This is me.

"No? Why no?" This is the driver. "You want 105 Central Park West."

I am an idiot. "No, no! Did I say *Central* Park West? Sorry, sorry! *Prospect* Park West, I meant Prospect Park West, 105 *Prospect* Park West."

"Oh, oh. Is okay."

Screeeeeeeech.

The driver pulls an impromptu U-turn. We are no longer get-ting on the BQE.

As we wait our turn at the animal clinic, a teenage girl walks in hugging a cat. Correction: The cat is hugging her. No freak-out, no frenzy—the girl simply holds the large untroubled tabby against her bosom as he extends his front legs toward her shoul-ders, a claw-sheathed paw on either side of her neck.

"Look." I nudge Jason. "A hugger."

Jason smiles, and I know he's thinking of his boy Iggy, whom he transports around our house in similar fashion.

The veterinarian has a Loo-zee-anna accent, a lackadaisical manner, and the long, lanky build of a retired basketball player. He's nice, examining Axl—meek and resigned on the table—checking her ears, her eyes, her teeth, her gums. He reckons her to be about a year old and in reasonably good health on visual assessment. "Could test her for FIV and leukemia, but if you're just going to turn her out I wouldn't bother," he says.

I get a little ripple at "turn her out." Isn't that the phrase for what a fancy man does to a fledgling whore?

"Give her a rabies shot, though; that'd be good."

We leave Axl in his care and return to fetch her around four. The waiting room is surprisingly hopping for New Year's Dusk. A dreadlocked receptionist calls the car service for us, and we chat with him as we settle up (the Muffin's certificate does not include the rabies shot, antibiotics booster, and general checkup), telling him of our kitten conundrum.

"*Kittens*? Excuse me, *kittens*?" A small, frail woman in baggy sweats and the same winged hairdo I wore in 1978 has been eavesdropping, and she can contain herself no longer. She says "kittens" as if pronouncing the name of the Messiah. "Did you say you have *kittens*?"

Cool, I think. *Someone wants to hear about our kittens. Maybe someone who wants our kittens!* "Yes," I tell her. "We have four; they're darling!"

The woman bobs her head, wings soldered in place with Aqua Net. "Yes, oh yes. I love kittens!"

This is too easy. "But they're sort of still a little feral." I sort of still have a conscience, sort of still place a little value in truth. "But the mother is tame—we brought her in to get fixed."

"I love cats, too," the winged woman reveals. "I take care of them. No kittens, though, not lately."

Jason has stepped back. This is his first encounter with a crazy cat lady (I don't count, damn it!) and he elects to have it from a safe distance.

"Oh?" I ask. "That's cool. How many?"

The lady beams. "Thirty-eight."

I take a step back myself. "Wow!" I say. "Thirty-eight! Gee . . . how many inside?"

She looks at me as though this is an unusual question. "Thirty-eight," she replies.

Just then an aggravated vet tech enters the waiting room, holding our borrowed carrier. "Somebody here to claim an Axl Rose?"

"Yes!" I say, relieved on several levels.

"Yeah? Well, don't worry, we cleaned her up," the tech says, "but just thought I'd let you know that for an encore, Axl decided to mosh in her own poop."

Between flutes of Veuve Clicquot, I pop downstairs to the bathroom where Axl recovers from hysterectomy and humiliation. The carrier is in the bathtub, and while I've left the wire door ajar and spread a towel in the tub, she continues to crouch in the back of the carrier. When she's post-op enough for food and water, I proffer some, but she declines. I feel awful—Jason and I have dined on lobster. I douse my culpability with more champagne.

Feral cat literature recommends keeping a post-op female indoors for three days, but the vet said we could let her go after forty-eight hours, and Axl is so miserable we decide to loose her sooner rather than later. Jason and I bring her out in the carrier as the kittens gather menacingly. We open the latch, swing wide the door—and Axl hurtles out like a raging bull from a rodeo chute, charging through our yard and that of our neighbors, the Hinkleys, racing over the ivy like a Nike ad, a swooshing blur of stripes, and out of sight.

While I'm secure in the knowledge that she now shares her kittens' poor opinion of me, when I go outside pss-pss-pssing a few hours later, Axl emerges, delicately catwalks my way, and sniffs my outstretched fingers. Then she head-butts my hand, inviting me to pet her. I have been absolved. For the first time all that stuff about "doing the right thing" finally resonates. Axl really will be better off not having two or three litters a year. My marriage will be better off not having to contend with two or three litters a year. And as I sit on the bucket, rubbing Axl under the chin, I realize what else will benefit from doing the right thing. Our community.

Does that sound unlikely from a cynical little snot like me? Yeah, well, there it is. I am coming to grasp a concept that eluded me throughout my adult life, residing as I did in anonymous Manhattan and Los Angeles apartments. I had sought that anonymity, craved and savored it. Come on; don't say you can't relate. You work all day among people you may not especially care for yet need be civil to or nothing gets done, but the minute you exit the employment environment you're halfway to blissful solitude. Even smushed up against countless others in a rush-hour train, you can—are expected to—keep your eye contact and language to a bare minimum; a muttered "excuse me" if you step on a toe is all that's required. Then you get off the subway and pop into the deli or the drugstore or the cheese shop or whatever purveyor supplies your essentials for the night, and while permitted to say "hi" and/or "thank you" to the clerk, you don't have to, nor does the clerk have to say "hi" and/or "you're welcome" to you. Now, home stretch, you're on your block, passing neighbors to whom you may or may not nod and no one is going to report you to the politesse police for your head-ducked, elbows-flared, aerobic trajectory to your building.

That had been my modus operandi. It began to alter slightly when Jason and I became an item, and he became a regular fixture on my erstwhile Manhattan street. Neighbors I vaguely recognized by sight he knew formally by name—not their names, maybe, but their dogs' names. There was Bagel, the beagle walked by the impatient yuppie. Honey, the Yorkie who hung out with the white-haired dude on a stoop a few buildings up from mine. Burberry, the nattily dressed wirehaired terrier who matched his nattily dressed owner, except the owner wore thick-framed eyeglasses and the dog did not. Soon I, too, was smiling at these people and stopping to briefly pass the time of day with their dogs.

But being back in Brooklyn gave my sense of community a real kick in the pants. It was like, ohhhh, okay: Community equals neighborhood equals home, a place to belong and contribute. Jason quickly introduced himself around, and I shyly learned who was who in his wake: The Hinkleys next door. Mr. Felipe, our Spanish teacher. Mr. Perez, the octogenarian "mayor" of the block. The Hernandezes, with their four beautiful daughters. Della and Linda across the street. Even our own gang of stoop thugs, led by a boulder-beaked, stooped-shouldered goon named Lucas.

Beyond "good morning" and *"buenas dias"* I began volunteering at the nearby library—my teen writers' workshop: Rebeca, Coral, Jade, Sammi, and Julez. Through their poems and stories and dreams, I reconnected with what it means to be a Brooklyn girl—

that thrust of hip, that twist of lip, that roll of eyes uniquely ours; that way we have of slapping a boy we like on the arm; that narrow, even stare that says *Do . . . not . . . mess.* The rhyme I composed to recite in my head as I sashay through *my* community goes like this:

> *My name is Nina, and I'm from Sunset.*
> *Live in a brownstone, not in a Quonset*
> *hut . . . Yeah I'm from Sunset.*
> *All right, what of it?*
> *If you don't like it,*
> *Then you can shove it.*

My community gave me my pride. How could I not give back to it?

With TNR, even if I get no farther than Axl, I'm doing my part to contain the feline infestation. It's nothing grandiose. Pat Kiernan, the drily appealing Canadian expat newscaster on New York 1, is not going to laud me as the channel's New Yorker of the Week, but if my shining moment of community service amounts to keeping local catshit to a minimum, I'm okay with that.

While I am getting all self-congratulatory, Iggy and Echo develop upper respiratory infections. She is sneezing—six, seven, eight sniffly explosions in a row—while he is oozing yellowish viscid gunk out of both eyes. To the vet, stat! Jason and I pack our babies into their nylon-and-mesh carrier—no easy fit. It is easy to be in denial that you have raised a fat cat till you try to cram him and his normal-sized sister into the same sack.

"Have they been undergoing any unusual stress lately?" asks their vet as he whips a thermometer out of Echo's ass. A rabbit-like, softly condescending fellow, he does not accept Muffin's certificates and ergo has dropped a notch or so in my esteem.

Damn, my scarlet letter must be sewn onto my other jacket. I have been philandering on Iggy and Echo with other cats, right in front of their eyes, blatantly cuckolding them. I explain to their vet about the ferals, saying in sum: "Iggy and Echo don't really like it—it makes them jealous and . . . and what you said about unusual stress."

"Oh?" He's probing Iggy's rectum now, and becomes a tad patronizing. "What makes you say that?"

"Well, they have a tendency to puff up like indignant blowfish and attack the kitchen windows," I retort. "Does that sound like a stress response to you?"

I am dangerously near offering the doc a taste of "that tone" when he flips the script to give us grief about Iggy's girth. The vet puts Iggy on the scale and to our chagrin we discover him to be sixteen pounds. That's sixteen pounds at eight months old. If big boy doesn't lose weight, we're informed, he'll be at risk for heart trouble, diabetes, and other physical banes. Jason shoots me a scolding look and I hang my head: I have been letting both cats lick off my ice cream spoon every night—nothing assuages a guilty conscience like treating the cats to dessert. Except it's not so much a treat anymore. They're like junkies— *Yo, what you got, man? Breyers, man? Edy's? You got the Turkey Hill? Whee, all right, Ben & Jerry's, the good shit!*—positioning themselves on the couch back, one on either side of my face, and if I don't give it up fast enough they smack me impatiently on the cheek.

Jason goes to the pet store and invests in low-cal kibble (which Iggy hates, and we soon abandon). He then heads for the basement and breaks out the power tools, coming up two hours later with his latest invention: a cat toy made from a dowel, a pull chain, and half a cheerleading pom-pom. If Iggy won't go on a diet, he'll go on an exercise program. Trouble is, the toy frightens Iggy—the grating sound of the pull chain and the gaudy flash of the flying pom-pom send him cowering under the table. Echo, however, takes a shine to it right off, leaping three feet in the air after her prey. Soon she learns the drawer where the toy is kept, and when she wants it will sit in front of the drawer and ask, "Mepp?" If one of us doesn't immediately oblige her, she will jump two feet and attach her claws to the handle of the closed drawer, trying to open it while frantically demanding, "Mepp! Mepp!" (Note to self: Remind Jason to get patent for Mepp.)

Meanwhile, I continue to spend way too much time outside. Jason grumbles about enrolling me in a 12-step program for crazy cat ladies, but while he plots an intervention I dig my heels in deeper. I am making progress. True, all four kittens still curse at the sight of me, and Sid and Nancy continue to avoid me like the plague. But Paul and Ray are coming around. When I dangle leftover soy-glazed salmon or chicken Florentine, they no longer feel compelled to bitch-slap it from my fingers—they now nibble it as courteously as star pupils at a finishing school. Paul has also gotten in on the game of stick—we're not the New York Rangers but we have fun.

Most amazingly, I have achieved fur-to-finger contact. While Ray has her snout in the kibble bowl, she will submit to several seconds of light petting between her shoulder blades. This is momentous, miraculous. This is Helen Keller signing W-A-T-E-R while Annie Sullivan pumps. This is Anwar Sadat and Menachem Begin at Camp David (thanks, Jimmy Carter!). This is the New York City teachers' union inking a contract. A very big deal, okay.

How could I possibly stop now?

chapter 7

aqualung

newsflash: paul wolke has no balls. Figuratively Paul Wolke has more balls than General Patton, Muhammad Ali, Insert Your Favorite Tough Guy Here. Literally, however, Paul Wolke is female. I know because now that Paul has warmed up to me a bit, her posture has changed. Specifically, her tail sticks up—the sign of a happy cat, or if not happy, nonthreatened. And what does one observe 'neath the erect tail of a kitten? Balls—small balls, but balls nonetheless—or, in the case of Paul Wolke, no balls at all.

Damn, that means one more ripening female in the mating matrix available to Bobby Darin, Homer Joy, and, eventually, an incestuous Sid Vicious. Sid hasn't yet given me the tail-high salute, and I know I was wrong about Paulie, but I still contend Sid is packing. Not nearly as belligerent as his runty sister, he nonetheless exudes a particular male vibe; he's that guy in school who hung back and didn't say much, insecure but smart enough to present a facade of cool. Kind of like Ryan on *The OC* (hey, I'm a teen culture professional, what's your excuse?).

Thank you for not shaking your head at how the extent of my obsession has led me to "give" the kittens personalities. If you're reading this you're no doubt cat-inclined and concur that cats have personalities. Unlike people who consider cats nothing more than dull, lima-bean-brained, love-withholding lumps, you know every cat has a complex and distinct disposition. If I tell you Ray Snarls is turning into the sweet and sassy coquette (no balls, I checked) we have come to call Raylene—a cat Reese Witherspoon or perhaps Cameron Diaz could play—you believe me unconditionally. Should I say Nancy Vicious is developing into a dippy airhead with vague potential to do harm—of the Juliette Lewis/ Brittany Murphy/Taryn Manning mold—you need no grains of salt. And when I point out that Paul Wolke—aka Cat of Chucky— would put casting agents in a quandary because they just don't write those kind of juicy roles for women, you nod, of course, mm-hmm. That doesn't mean I worry about her any less.

Especially over the next twenty-four hours.

The storm begins shortly before noon. It's Saturday, so I'm in the basement of the library with the writers' group, but we hear an announcement that due to snow the library will close at one. Cool! New Yorkers love a good blizzard; Brooklynites especially. Correction: We love the first day of the season's first blizzard. We love to sound off about how the mayor and the Department of Sanitation are going to handle this one; we love to compare it with blizzards past; we love to wager whether schools will close (even grown-ups root for the snow day).

Jason's band, the Vapours, have a show tonight. I have no plans to attend. What can I say, I'm a shoddy excuse for a rock 'n' roll wife. I spent the 1990s on the fringe of fabulous, writing about music from lo-fi obscure to obscenely immense, and by now I am pretty much rocked out. I have seen so many acts in so many settings that the fact that I am not completely deaf is among the miracles of the ages. Naturally if someone handed me tickets to Nick Cave or Robyn Hitchcock or Neil Young or Willie Nelson (which they no longer do) I'd muster up the enthusiasm and mascara required.

But the Vapours? Don't get me wrong, they're a good band, a fun band, a little loose in spots but they have the tunes and that's what counts. And I do want to be supportive of my dear one's art—it's not that I never go to the show. I see them occasionally. When it's not at a million o'clock in the morning. Or in some godforsaken section of Hipsterville so hip the hipsters don't even know it's there yet. I sit at a table by myself, or with Rosemary or Gini or whoever else I can get to come—I don't for God's sake *wiggle* in front of the stage (which, except for the strip club they sometimes play, usually isn't a stage, but a corner by the men's room, or the place where the pool table goes when it's not a live music night). And after the gig, I don't go around with a Composition notebook and pen, eagerly inviting the audience members who are not already friends of the band if they'd like to sign the Vapours mailing list.

Now, with a blizzard bearing down, I have a good excuse to stay home in my pajamas. If only I could think up an argument to convince Jason that he doesn't want to truck out to some dive in Greenpoint, which no doubt is beginning to resemble Greenland by now. Thank goodness for Ashley—Vapours bass player, band driver, and general voice of reason. While stuck in traffic on the BQE she kills time by calling up to cancel the gig. That leaves only the welfare of ferals to obsess about in this weather. Will the shelter hold up? It's designed to minimize air entry and maximize body heat, but how could it not be freezing in there? It looks so flimsy, and it's feather-light (there's a brick on the roof to keep it from blowing away). With the shelter standing twelve inches high and twelve to fourteen inches of precipitation predicted, a burial at snow seems likely.

Jason and I spend the evening watching flakes fall. A neighbor across the street who's been shoveling his steps and sidewalk on a half-hourly schedule eventually gets to Jason, who begins a losing battle of his own. I have an exercise in futility, too, trying to keep the cat shack from disappearing. Axl and company seem snug enough whenever I check on them. They'd probably prefer me to stem the neurosis and cease and desist from shining a flashlight into the cat shack entrance every five minutes. Sometime between ten and eleven I look out the kitchen window one more time, note that the cats have gotten their igloo after all, and go to bed.

The next morning I bundle up and head out to do my share of shoveling. I haven't shoveled snow in decades, but I used to help my dad when I was little. Well, I don't know how much help I actually was, and I can't remember enjoying it at the time, but looking back on it makes me smile. Now I am a landlady; it is among my responsibilities. Naturally, I have my priorities straight and forsake bipeds in favor of quadrupeds, taking my shovel out back first, to dig out the cat shack, where there's barely a speck of doorway visible.

Oh, by the way, it's real pretty out. But far better writers than I have described their share of winter wonderlands and we all know how not competitive I am, so I won't go there. Instead I'll tell you how god-like it feels to know there are beings on this planet—beings with brains the size of you-know-whats, but still—

who believe me omnipotent enough to have caused the blizzard. Because the way the kittens come shooting out of the shack, all puffed-up pissy, fussy, and hungry as hell, it's clear they think this is all my fault.

Once a path from the door of our house to the door of theirs has been cleared, and the kibble bowls unburied and filled, the ferals decide that maybe this snow stuff is not so bad. Axl returns to the shelter—and I to the kitchen—but the kittens, having spent nearly a full day cooped up, go into banzai extreme-sports mode. Eurotrash X-heads at Ibiza disco foam parties have nothing on the furbags. They chase each other clumsily through the drifts, powder flying as they tumble, then take to the trees. Jason comes downstairs, pours coffee, and joins me at the window in time to see Sid, Nancy, Ray, and Paul swinging from the branches of the rose of Sharon like lunatic Japanese lanterns. Keep your *America's Next Top Model,* your *Trading Spouses,* your *Entourage.* We have Cat-TV.

"Cute, huh?" I have such a flair for the obvious.

"Yes, they are very cute," Jason says, trying not to be grumpy. He tends toward grump in the morning, but Flying Karamozov Kittens are a good tonic for grump.

We watch the kittens for another minute as they climb, dangle and plummet, race, chase and somersault.

"Okay," I say—to my husband, the window, the cats outside, the cats inside, myself. "Let's see who lives through the winter . . ."

Little do I suspect that our wild world is about to get wilder.

Super Bowl Sunday. Not that I even know who's playing. What I do know is people in rec rooms across the country are banding together in red-blooded us-versus-them spirit to yell at their television sets—and I want a piece. It doesn't happen often but there are times when I feel strongly compelled to be "normal." So as Jason, Ashley, and her drummer boyfriend, Rich—collectively known as the Vapours—rehearse in the music room (originally, I presume, a dining room, now devoted to recording equipment and band gear), I get busy on guacamole and spinach enchiladas and shrimp in chipotle sauce. For some reason I confuse Super Bowl Sunday with Cinco de Mayo. Rosemary arrives in time for dinner. No one has so much as looked at the spectacle in cleats—we're not *that* normal, we have no interest in yelling at athletes. To us the main event is the halftime show. We want to yell as this evening's appointed dinosaur rocker or popular hip-hopper or newly arrived diva embarrasses him-/herself, and perhaps be offended by the colossal advertising budgets blown in a thirty-second commercial or two.

Before I feed my guests, I tend to the furbags. Their hissing and spitting at the sight of me has largely abated—I can enter the backyard without being heckled like Céline Dion opening for Rancid—so as the motion-detector bulb flicks on I feel fully at ease and in my element. I take a head count. Okay, here's Axl . . . and Sid and Nancy . . . where's Ray? all right, here she is . . . and pushy Paulie, a few seconds late for dinner, sticking her snout into every bowl before choosing one.

But what the . . . ? What is that—*who* is that—scrumping around among the decomposing leaf piles and half-melted snow mounds of the Hinkley spread? One of the baby daddies, surely—although now that Axl's been spayed they haven't been lurking much. I look toward the sound.

Scrump, scrump . . . scrump, scrump . . .

Something is lumbering amid the shadows and left-out lawn furniture. I've never been inside the Hinkley house, but judging from their yard I suspect they got a touch of the Sanford gene. It looks like an abandoned tag sale or an end-of-season blowout at Thos. Baker—benches, lounges, tables and chairs; a state-of-the-art barbecue grill, an enormous speaker abandoned after one of their summer deejay parties; flowerpots of all sizes; assorted wind chimes, pedestals, hanging baskets, and what I can only list as "random decorative items." There's even a sort of gazebo-trellis thingee for an anorectic wisteria that never met the challenge of the climb and, inexplicably, a large piece of wood or pasteboard painted with an early American flag. And tonight, tonight there's something else out there—something animate . . . something that scrumps.

"Pss-pss-pss?" I venture. Glancing back I notice the ferals hovering frozen over their food. Just then the motion-detector light goes off since, after all, everyone is motionless. Everyone in our yard, that is. In the Hinkleys' yard the scrumping continues unabated. Okay, I'm starting to get scared. There is no effective barrier between our block's backyards and those of the next block over, and not to be rude but that block is a ghetto block—aluminum-siding private houses and shady apartment buildings and regularly scheduled drug busts. *"My name is Nina/And I'm from Sunset . . . ,"* I rap in my head for courage.

"Kitty . . . ?" I call hoarsely, through a suddenly dry throat.

Scrump, scrump . . .

"Kitty . . . ?" Whoever he is, he's huge—I'm talking big enough to intimidate Crocodile Dundee—but all I can really decipher is an amorphous shape, low to the ground. "Nice kitty . . . ?"

Finally the nice kitty lifts his head to face me. And his eyes are glowing red. I stumble back a step, kicking the motion-detector bulb into action. It casts enough light for me to see what is either the biggest cat I've ever seen . . . or . . . not a cat . . . Holy crap! Raccoon!

Okay, those of you smirking, cut it out. I am from Brooklyn, damn it. To me wildlife is pigeons, cockroaches, subway rats. Raccoons most definitely are in the province of PBS's *Nature*. Raccoons are exotic animals; raccoons are freakin' fauna, all right—I have seen them in a zoo. What is it doing here? (Um, not much, actually—just staring at me with laser-pointer eyes.) How did it get here? I recall Jason's report on his amble through historic Greenwood Cemetery—the biggest boneyard in the five boroughs. A guard, desperate for nonspectral company, gave him a ride, tour-guiding the highlights (for instance, the monument to a gunned-down Mafia princess bride, which depicts her getting whacked on cathedral steps in lurid marble detail). The guard also edified Jason on the cemetery's animal population, which includes raccoons in no small numbers. But Greenwood's a good mile from our house, and I simply cannot fathom a raccoon strolling down Fifth Avenue or catching the B-63 bus.

"Guys . . . ?" I say. By *guys* I mean my husband and friends inside, not the cat statues at my feet. "Guys?" They have got to see this! I back up, forcing the kittens to scatter lest I stomp them. I bang on the storm door without taking my eyes off the enormous bushy bandit. *"Guys! Guys! Raccoon! Raccoon!"* I gibber madly.

Ashley and Rich are remarkably blasé, but Jason, armed with flashlight, and Rosemary come busting outside.

"Where's a raccoon, what're you talking about raccoon?" Rosemary doesn't believe me.

Of course my ruckus—and the yappy barking of a nosy nearby dog—has put the raccoon on the move; he is in the process of slowly climbing a spindly tree. I point this out.

"Holy crap, that's a raccoon all right," Rose says.

"Honey? Honey! Do you see him?" I am yanking on Jason's sleeve. Jason has been all too silent, and I know what he's thinking—he's thinking he prefers a colony of cats to a brood or flock or school of raccoons "The raccoon? Do you? See him?"

"I sure do," he says. "That's one bigass raccoon." Jason is not nearly as excited as I am. He has not only seen raccoons before, he has, in his youth, gone out into the woods with assorted kinfolk to stalk and shoot them, and . . . do what with them I have no idea, nor do I want to know, but there is no Daniel Boone hat among his belongings.

"You know," says Rosemary, gearing up to pontificate. "You don't want to try befriending it. Raccoons are carnivorous, and they can be vicious, due to the blah-blah-blah . . ."

I love the girl to pieces, but she does have a tendency to come off like Cliff Clavin, her Boston accent only part of it.

"Yo, shut up! Goddamn it, shut up already, you hear me!" This comment is directed at the yappy dog in the nearby yard, and is made, presumably, by the yappy dog's owner. The dialogue that transpires next could take place only in Brooklyn. Or possibly parts of New Jersey . . .

"That your dog?" Rosemary's voice carries. "I'll tell you why he's barking—there's this big raccoon over here."

A big male voice booms back. "What? What are you talking?"

"Raccoon!" we all shout.

"What?"

"Raccoon! There's a raccoon in this tree . . ."

"Shut up, raccoon. There's no raccoon over there!"

"There is." Rosemary does not back down, even from unseen adversaries. "It's a raccoon, I'm telling you!"

"It *ain't* no raccoon; *I'm* telling *you*!"

"Yeah? You think you know something? You want to tell me what I'm looking at here?"

"Yeah, I'll tell you . . ."

"So tell me . . ."

"Your mother!"

The halftime show is anticlimactic after such potentially rabid commotion. As we settle in for dinner, conversation turns to cooking. Ashley—who is lean, petite, and possessed of a deadpan humor—regales us with a tale of her Korean grandmother's infatuation with Frugal Gourmet/accused sex offender Jeff Smith. (Ten men claimed Smith molested them while working as teenage assistants in his Tacoma, Washington, restaurant in the 1970s; Smith was never arrested, and settled out of court for about five million dollars.) "She's very loyal to him. Even after it came out he was a diddler," Ashley says. "Even after he died. She'll talk about him like, 'Yeff Smeef does this,' or 'Yeff Smeef says that,' and I'll be, 'Grandma, Jeff Smith is dead, he died, he's dead.' And she'll get very angry and insist 'Yeff Smeef not dead!'"

You had to be there—and smoke the pot there and drink the beer there—to find this as hilarious as we do. But "Yeff Smeef not dead!" becomes our rallying cry for the rest of the night.

And beyond.

Seeing as how my husband is Jason G. Sanford, he has great difficulty throwing anything away. The thing I want dispensed with is a "kitty condo"—you know, those large carpeted toilet paper rolls with holes cut into the side. Our kitty condo was donated by my mom's neighbor the day we got Iggy and Echo. Clearly, Jason and I failed to pass along our appreciation for the gently used to our cats, as Iggy and Echo would have nothing to do with a pre-owned clubhouse. They've been avoiding it for about six months now, and I want it tossed, but Jason must do this in stages. He brings it from the living room to the hallway, stores it in the basement for a few days, then keeps it in the hallway for a few more days, and finally it goes out. Just not in the garbage. Not yet. Jason puts it inside our front gate.

The day after Super Bowl Sunday, someone moves into it.

I spy him as I dart a scornful glance at the condo on my way out to work. He is on the lower "floor" and he isn't moving and he isn't mewing. All I can see is a whitish nose, some crusty whiskers, eyes narrowed at three-quarter mast.

"Who are you?" I ask.

The cat doesn't answer.

I go back inside, fill some Chinese food containers (aka Jewish Tupperware) with kibble and water, and place them by the condo. Big mistake.

The cat is still there in the evening, and it would appear that he hasn't budged a hair, except that some of the cat food has been eaten and, subsequently, regurgitated a few inches from the condo. *Lovely*, I think, sidestepping vomit. "What's the matter, dude? Not feeling so hot?"

The cat doesn't answer.

Next morning a little more kibble is gone, and adjacent to the vomit is poop. This is unheard of. Cats do *not* shit where they eat. The cat in the condo must be very sick, very perverse, or both. I think it's time for him to move it on down the road. I rattle the cage—a euphemism for kick the condo. Gently, of course; just a tap. And out he darts. The ugliest cat I have ever laid eyes on.

He's the color of pus, the color of cancer, an infection with fur. He is, or was at one time, mostly white. Even his eyes—this is the creepy part—where they should be amber or green are a cloudy, filthy white. This cat hasn't groomed since the Clinton administration. There's the odd patch of displaced tabby on his rump and flank. His nose is running. He's skinny. He makes a possum look attractive, a scorpion seem cuddly. As he exits the condo he does so in a crouch, ringed tail dragging. He doesn't go far, just scoots out the gate and huddles by the garbage cans. I stand watching this pathetic, barely living thing for a few seconds before gathering some of the advertising flyers tucked into the iron banister to clean up the poop and puke. But I leave the food, water, and condo where they are.

"Aqualung, my friend, don't you start away uneasy . . . ," I pre-eulogize the appalling furbag. I figure he'll be dead by sundown. That's what I tell Jason when we discuss his condition from our respective desks that afternoon. While I don't relish discovering a stiffening corpse at our gate, I figure a cat who shits where he eats is not long for this world.

Yet there he is, still breathing. I call Jason, who is working late. "Guess what?" I say. "Yeff Smeef not dead."

"Damn . . ." Jason evicts Yeff Smeef from the kitty condo upon his return, throws the thing (condo, not kitty) into the garbage receptacle, then tosses the Chinese food containers on top. *That ought to do it,* he thinks.

Come morning, condo gone, Yeff Smeef not dead. Yeff Smeef, curled in the corner where the condo had been, still, in fact, able to manage bodily functions in abominably distasteful manner. I exclaim things like "scat!" and "shoo!" but am concerned—I've learned cats are loath to leave the site of a food source, which means I fear Yeff Smeef will stay in that exact spot, growing more repulsive and wretched, till he finally expires. Fortunately, following a few kibble-less days, Yeff Smeef takes the hint and slinks off.

In the wake of his disappearance, though, comes an ominous strangeness: The air is askew, the light less light, the dark more dark. It makes me nervous, like I evoked some bad juju. Remember, just because you're paranoid doesn't mean evil spirits aren't out to get you. Especially in Sunset, where it is not uncommon to dig up bugaboo Voodoo Mason jars. And Yeff Smeef is a true son of Sunset—goblin, troll, chupacabra, maybe the devil himself.

When Jason awakens me around 1 AM the following night—a February night, half-mooned and full-on freezing—the superstitious part of me believes Yeff Smeef has had his vengeance.

chapter 8

how to trap a feral cat *in one* easy lesson

i am running down the stairs,

I am choking on my heart—no, I am choking on the smoke, smoke thick as goo, as pudding, a substance, gushing into the hall from a ceiling vent. I am pulling on my coat, spontaneously weeping but nothing—no noise, no tears—comes out. Jason is on with 911, but someone else—who? where?—has already made the call. I hear the alarms with my spine, my spleen, my past, my previous life, as the trucks pull up. Engine company. Ladder company. Neighbors in topcoats and pajama bottoms, looking up. It's the night after Yeff Smeef's banishment and the half-commercial, half-residential structure adjacent to our house is on fire. Only I don't see any fire—just firefighters. Many firefighters in full gear pounding up our front steps armed with axes. They are yelling, "Who's in there?" and "Anyone in there?" and "We need to get in there!"

My voice will not work. The firefighters are fixing to gain entry with their axes. Why, why? I don't see any fire. Our house isn't on fire; our house is on smoke. The Sixpack Sisters aren't roasting in their beds. I'm sure of it. It's Saturday night, they're party girls, and even with the earplugs I wear to sleep I'm always roused by their door slams and boot clops. Why is this happening? Why won't my vocal cords obey? When I finally kick-start them, the feel is scream but the sound is mew. "Wait! Please! Keys!" Sentences. Impossible. Besides, I don't have any keys; I have fled the house with . . . what, a hair clip. No wallet, no last will and testament, no laptop, and definitely no keys. "Please! Husband! Keys!"

"You better get 'em lady, and get 'em fast!"

Seven minutes have elapsed since Jason shook me awake. Or seven seconds, seven hours. I collide with him at the gate. "Keys!" I gasp. "Firemen! Upstairs!"

Now there are firefighters in the upstairs apartment, flinging, I imagine, the Sixpack Sisters' crap out of the roof access nook they promised not to use as a closet. Now there are firefighters on our roof. Now more, racing through the ground floor of our house, to get to the yard. Now there are cops, too; two cops in uniform, a man and a woman, stocky, dark-haired, expressionless. Now there are more neighbors gaping—gaping at no fire. But where is Jason? "Our cats!" he tells the cops. "You have to let me go inside; I have to get our cats!"

I am useless. I am stupefied. I am a Weeble. I toddle after Jason. "Cats . . . ," I croak. Smoke is everywhere. My eyes are fully functional now, streaming. Jason has corralled the cats in the music room but has no clue where the carrier is. This I know! This I can do! I dig it out and we shove Iggy and Echo, who are not remotely freaked out, inside. "Okay, you got them, now get out of here," the lady cop says.

I don't give a second's thought to the cats outside. Thought, in general, eludes me.

The ladder company makes its assault against the burning building, the building burning with no flame. Is this weird, that I would see no bright orange indisputable evidence that something terribly wrong is going on in there? That's when windows start smashing. And smashing and smashing. Finally, smoke begins to spew, every conceivable evil unleashed from Pandora's broken-open glass box. It's as though the smoke is afraid of the fire, fleeing the fire, escaping in a panic, in a stampede. And still I have to trust there's a fire going on—still I do not see a flicker. This is probably a good thing.

My fingers find the hair clip in my pocket, gouge the teeth of the clip into the meaty part of my palm, dull plastic teeth with no bite. More firefighters are now axing their way into the Hinkley house next to ours. I can't imagine why, but I hear someone opine that firefighters need to explore several houses to see where the smoke stops. There are a lot of people gathered around—this is an event, a block anti-party—observing and exchanging comments about fire. It's like they're watching a movie, except they're standing up and permitted to talk. The voices of neighbors come at me like will-o'-the-wisps, some indecipherable, others clear as chimes. The Hinkley tenant who is at home must be highly resistant to commotion; she must sleep with earplugs made of lead. She is outside now, blinking in her fuzzy slippers.

The young couple and their small children who live—lived— in the burning apartment stand together in a clump. I don't know them. They live right next door and I don't know them; they look like so many of the dark-eyed, flat-featured people who trundle down the avenue with multiple baby strollers and cell phones. They are solemn and still; their eyes are large, their mouths are slack. I am repeating "oh my God" over and over, but they are mum, even the kids, nary a sniffle. One of them had a huge plush Tweety Bird toy I could see from our yard, a stuffed yellow light-bulb in their window. Tweety's fire fodder now.

As I babble on the sidewalk, I'm approached by Sasha, the eldest of the lovely Hernandez daughters. The Hernandezes live a few doors down, and they're all outside watching, even the lit-tlest daughter, a kindergartner, who hovers by their front gate—a fire must be rated G. Sasha tells me we can put Iggy and Echo in their house. She leads the way. The Hernandezes have an ancient toy-sized terrier; the terrier is hysterical; we keep Iggy and Echo in their carrier, in a separate room from the delirious dog. Out-side again, Sasha offers me a seat on their stoop. She brings me a blanket, arranges it around my shoulders. She brings me a glass of water. With ice. She tells me not to worry—we are safe. I thank her and look at the glass of water and wonder how it got in my hand. Oh, right, Sasha. Sasha is almond-eyed and smoothly, nat-urally dirty blond and in control. *Her name is Sasha/And she's from Sunset* . . . She is sixteen years old.

A taxicab gets as far up our street as it can. The Sixpack Sisters disembark and teeter up the block in Saturday-night-special footwear. One of them has on a white coat with a feathery collar. Her straight black hair and the collar like sea anemones blow about her face and throat; several layers of mascara rim her small, slate eyes, and there's a frosty pastel on her thin, tight lips; she looks epic and beautiful and terrifying, Angel of Death–ish. She lights a long, white cigarette and crosses her arms against her chest to smoke it.

A cat comes tearing out of a house. Whose house? Our house? Whose cat? Which cat? I'm reminded about the cats—those other cats, the outside cats, where are they, how are they? "Hey!" someone cries. "You see that cat?"

The cat runs under a car. The firefighters fight the fire. They do so for hours. Throughout it all I do not see a single lick of flame.

We are the luckiest people and cats ever, ever, ever. The interior of the building next door is ravaged, but there's virtually no damage to our house, our things, except for the smell. It's a dry, sinister smell, a mocking aftermath, insidious rather than in your face. It smells how choking on a small hair feels. Not so bad as a smell, but the connotation of the smell—that's what's bad. The smell says: *Get you next time.* And depending on the weather, or the time of day, or some other factor that is beyond me, in certain spots—open a closet door, turn a corner—it will continue to smell for months to come, despite our washing down the walls with a water-and-baking-soda solution.

But we are fine. I'm embarrassed. I did not function particularly well. I don't know how I managed to not pass out on the sidewalk. If I had seen fire, seen anything orange for that matter, I would've done just that. I have been "good in a crisis" before—the incident of Jason's kick in the head comes to mind—but in this crisis I was a listing balloon, I was a rag stuck to a tree branch, I was a used toothpick, simultaneously brittle and wet.

And yet we are fine. The building next door is brick; it's standing—the inside I can only imagine, and don't. Its yard, never a candidate for *House & Garden,* now looks like a war zone. Broken glass, twisted metal, shards of trashed fence, detritus from inside the apartments and offices mingle with stubborn filthy snow and mud. Except for frayed bits of picket lying willy-nilly, our yard looks the same. Our cat house, and our Rubbermaid garbage can that serves as the cat house annex, and our—have I done this before, actually claimed them, referred to them as *ours?*—our ferals are all okay.

That cat I saw hurtling out onto the street during the fire may have been a figment of my imagination. But these cats—Axl and her kittens—are alive and well, no worse for wear. Or so it appears. Cats, as you may have witnessed, can front. When they slip and splat on the dismount of a miscalculated leap, for instance, their manner is always *I meant to do that.* It could be that inside they still quake over all those firefighters with asbestos attitude and heavy boots, but outside, the surface is implacable, persuasively so. The wreckage of the yard next door certainly agrees with the kittens. It's a veritable Disneyland of crap to climb up and hide in, and they go for it with manic glee. They chase each other up and down and through the rubble, scattering ash, collecting soot on their coats.

Unlike Axl, who is completely unfazed, I'm having aftershocks, ripples of trembles. She is chill, sidles up for affection and watches her kittens with enigmatic eyes—she and Sid have the same eyes, the same betray-nothing stare.

Then three, maybe four days post-fire, she is gone.

There is only one rational explanation for this. Alien abduction. Beamed up to the mother ship. Sucked into the extraterrestrial vortex.

What, you got something better? Please, do share. Hit by a car? Street cats get hit by cars; yard cats have no mechanical predators. Slaughtered by a bigger, stronger, faster beast? Not without a fight, and I would have heard something, smelled something, found something—partially digested remains, one streaky bloodied paw print on the cat shack wall. Wandered off in search of a more reliable food source? Come on, there is no more reliable food source—I'm out there like clockwork with quality kibble and table scraps. A day, two days, three, I wait for her stoic expression and arched-back, stiff-legged yoga postures on the windowsill, then I tell myself to give it up. Axl Rose has left the venue. She has pulled a permanent McCavity. She isn't coming back.

A friend of mine had two cats, and when one died the survivor mourned in a box for two months and lost four pounds. I know that Iggy would mourn Echo and she would mourn him (albeit less vocally). But those stone-hearted Teflon-coated kittens outside? Grief does not enter their repertoire. Again I could be misinterpreting the feline mystique, but as far as I can tell they're like, *Whatever, man—more kibble for us.* I sit on my bucket to give Raylene, sweetest of Axl's offspring, a tentative stroke and wonder how she cannot miss her mommy.

The disappearance of Axl Rose. It sounds like the title of a V. C. Andrews paperback, and it haunts me fittingly, her absence carving its own alcove in my rambling internal manor of loss. (If your psyche doesn't have a rambling manor of loss, let me just say you're saving a bundle in emotional real estate tax.) Yet it's as though the kittens have turned into instant teenagers now that the mama cat's away. Roaming farther, absent longer, probably experimenting with drugs.

For optimal feral scoping I need to check from the upstairs windows, which provide a broader vista. Occasionally I will spy Nancy several backyards away performing a balance-beam routine, one paw placed neatly after the other along one fence picket after the other. Or I'll watch Paul Wolke compete in the championship squirrel-chasing event high in the boughs of a distant maple. Like our Olympics, the Feral Olympics take place in various venues and arenas, no longer limited to our property and the two adjacent lots. I am becoming accustomed to this. True, I do worry when one of them takes off for a full day (especially Ray—Paul has that Panzer tank mentality; Nancy has Sid to protect her, they roll as a duo). But I don't completely spazz out the way I did when convinced they were slain by a ruthless Bobby Darin. And when they are around, I'm comforted by the crunch of kibble in quadraphonic sound.

So just as I start getting used to a four-feral outpost populated by free-range juvenile delinquents, whom do I spy one day dipping into the kibble trough? Oh no! It can't be. Please, Lord, let it not be so. Make it another candidate for *Extreme Feline Makeover*. A confrontation is imminent. The hunched, hungry figure is startled by the click of the turning lock; he seems to lunge in place. But he stands his ground when I step into the yard, lifting his eyes to give me the stare-down. Oh, Jesus. Those eyes. Those worm-white, black-slit, gelid eyes. Yeff Smeef! Not dead, no, not dead at all. Instinctively (okay, maybe not instinctively, maybe for dramatic effect) I peel back my lips and bare my teeth, and if I could flatten my ears any closer to the sides of my head I would. Thusly composed, I hiss, *"WHI-I-I-I-I-I-I-H!"*

Yeff Smeef regards me, malevolent as warm mayonnaise.

"You freak!" I say aloud. Then I take a loud stomp forward, and Yeff Smeef skulks off a few yards. Any satisfaction I get from this is fleeting, since as soon as I return to my corner my opponent advances to eat his fill. Unfair! This is what will fill the void left by Axl Rose? An attractive, amiable animal replaced by Rumpelstiltskin, Snidely Whiplash, Baby Doc? Ew!

Okay, fine, it's true: I'm shallow in my feline fancy, I can cop to that. I only like cats who've had the decency to lick themselves in the last hour, or year. Go ahead, remind me that puking and pooping on my doorstep were involuntary bodily functions, that Yeff Smeef has never deliberately done anything evil to me. Aha, here I must counter—he's done nothing I can prove with ironclad evidence. Yet I beseech you, consider the chronology: (1) We exorcise him from the front of the house. (2) An invisible conflagration ensues (which the fire department chalks up to the faulty electrics of a space heater like they always do). (3) Axl Rose becomes the object of an ET autopsy. (4) Yeff Smeef insinuates himself in the backyard. Coincidence? Give me a break! Something wicked this way came, and you can't convince me otherwise.

I load a water gun. This is war.

See, it's not just him eating our kibble and drinking our water and being so mangy and dissolute and butt-ugly that bothers me. This is not about me being miserly, or easily aesthetically offended. I know Yeff Smeef's dastardly plan: He's waiting for our females to go into heat so he can plant his demon seed! It's time to get serious about TNR.

Neighborhood Cats holds a seminar once a month, an AP class in feral control and maintenance. After a conversation or two with a kind and patient Neighborhood Cats employee named Meredith, I sign up. The seminar is held in a conference room at the ASPCA, on Manhattan's Upper East Side. Fifteen people in attendance. All races, all ages, both genders, and every borough except Staten Island represents. The only person who seems out of place is this young mook, the spitting image of Vinnie Barbarino, until it's revealed that he's here with his girlfriend and his girlfriend's sister. Talk about pussy-whipped. In a keening Queens accent the girlfriend avows "Cats are my life," and I wonder how that makes the boyfriend feel. The sister agrees that cats are her life, too—the sisters are in service to more than a dozen ferals at their family home.

The sisters from Queens are not the only crazy cat ladies present. One heavyset brunette from the Bronx, no shame in her game, is quick to self-identify as such. "I'm one of those crazy cat ladies," she says in a smoker's voice. As if the sweatshirt emblazoned with the wispy airbrushed visage of a Siamese wasn't a dead giveaway. The other crazy cat lady—a willowy blonde of supermodel stature—doesn't say so straight up, but her cell phone tells all. The ring tone is the Meow Mix commercial, and she becomes so flustered when it goes off mid-seminar she has trouble turning it off, treating us to a good sixty seconds of "meow, meow, meow, meow . . . meow, meow, meow, meow . . ."

The rest of us are more moderate. The rest of us either made the mistake of emitting the entreaty "pss-pss-pss?" or are living with the results of that mistake made by others. For instance, the co-op board president whose building, rife with stray-coddling little old ladies, is now so infested with breeding furbags no one can sleep at night. We learn these things about one another's situations because we are asked to go around the table and explain our presence by the thin, intense-looking man, what's left of his dark hair closely cropped, who leads the seminar.

This is Bryan; screen name: headcat. An encounter with ferals in a vacant lot near his home led him to launch Neighborhood Cats in the late 1990s. Other people were obsessed with Y2K; Bryan had his hands full with TNR. Now running the organization is his full-time job. Since Neighborhood Cats introduced a resolute TNR advocacy and education program, euthanasia rates at city shelters have dropped substantially. Considering that it costs about sixty bucks to "put a cat to sleep," TNR saves NYC a good chunk of change.

Bryan distributes a copy of a 108-page handbook, *A Guide to Trap-Neuter-Return for the Feral Cat Caretaker*, and proceeds, over the next hour or so, to go through it with us chapter by chapter. We learn about developing community relations (how to inform neighbors that poisoning cats is a criminal offense for which they could go to prison). We learn about nutrition (we are encouraged to amp up provisions with vitamin C) and tricks for keeping ants and slugs at bay. ("What about raccoons?" asks the crazy cat lady from the Bronx. The Bronx is kiss-close to Westchester, and that's the wilderness as far as I'm concerned, so her raccoon problem does not surprise me.) We learn about constructing the Neighborhood Cats–approved shelter (I raise my hand and testify to what an excellent shelter it is) as well as less power-tool-intensive alternatives, such as the Rubbermaid storage-bin-*cum*-kitty-shanty. Eventually we get to what we all came to learn: how to trap a cat.

Bryan brings out a display model—a twelve-pound wire cage measuring thirty-six inches in length, twelve in width, and eleven in height, with a guillotine-style up-and-down sliding front door, a hook-shaped trigger, and a trip plate. It was not designed to be a cat trap per se; it's an all-around critter-catcher—raccoons, possums, varmints of that ilk. Bait trap with food, animal enters trap, animal steps on trip plate, and—voilà! To paraphrase the old Roach Motel slogan, "Critters check in but they don't check out."

Except, we are told, it is not always that simple. Cats, apparently, can be pretty cagey around cages. Because they are suspicious and resist the allure bait. Because they avoid—by strategy or dumb luck—engaging the trip plate, entering the trap to dine in style by stepping around it or leaning over it. Because they're *cats*; they have *ways*. Several pages of our handbooks are dedicated to outsmarting the hard-to-trap cat, including construction and operation of various alterna-traps such as the box trap, drop trap, door trap, trap-in-a-box, and, my particular favorite, the camouflage trap, which should be especially effective if your feral happens to be related to Rambo.

Despite these caveats I leave the seminar bursting with the righteous purpose of Elmer Fudd: I'm gonna twap a cat! What I can't quite wrap my conviction around is the mass-trapping method endorsed by Neighborhood Cats. I understand the logic to this MO over the one-cat-at-a-time approach, but even if I got four traps (five if you count Yeff Smeef, which I'd rather not), at about sixty-five bucks a pop, I don't have unlimited cat storage. Okay, there is the basement; I could easily fit four or five cages down there, but you know how I feel about the basement. Besides, I know how Jason—not to mention Iggy and Echo—would react to four or five ululating, urinating caged cats in any part of our house. So I'm leaning toward buying one trap and seeing how it goes—it simply feels more manageable.

Who will it be, I wonder, the first kitten tempted into the cage of mercy? My money's on Ray—she's the most inquisitive, least suspicious of the bunch. I hope so. I still haven't given up on transforming Ray Snarls into a bona fide lap cat. She not only has no problem with petting now, she seems to actually like it (as opposed to Paul, whom I can also pet, three times, before she whirls, hops away as if singed, and regards me with all the *Don't touch me! You don't know me! Don't you* dare *touch me!* disdain of Flip Wilson's Geraldine). With her chalk-and-soot coat and her blind marble eye Ray, dare I say it, is my friend; she's my girl. Even when I'm not crouching as low to the ground as possible, she is not afraid of me. I can walk around the yard without making her skitter for cover. In fact, she even follows me around with late-onset imprinting.

I wonder if she will continue to do so after today. Because today—this evening, before she even takes a bite of dinner—Ray elects to follow me into the house.

And proceeds to go completely ballistic.

The second the storm door closes behind her, she realizes what she has done and takes off down the hall. This is when I realize she has slipped in behind me—and that this is not good, not good at all. Iggy and Echo are in the kitchen, and they will not be amused. I flash on all the ills that might infect a feral—could Ray be lousy with FIV, feline leukemia, distemper, rabies, nits, worms, fleas, lice, each potential malaise eager to attach itself to the virgin immune systems of my house pets? (I am not an especially scrupulous person but I have taken pains to conscientiously wash up after every act of feral maintenance.) What's more, every door to every room is open; there are things to crawl behind where a kitten Ray's size could hole up interminably.

"Raaaaay!" I cry, running after her, hoping to head her off before she gets to the stairs. Fortunately she's so quick, before I even gain on her she's crashed into the front door and bounced off. Now she's speeding back the way she came, dust muffins pinwheeling at her heels. Iggy and Echo are alerted to the ruckus, and I chase them from the kitchen into the music room, shutting them in before Ray caroms off the washing machine and into the kitchen with a splat. She leaps onto one of the Formica tables, then flings herself, claws out, onto perhaps the most offensive piece of arts and crap decor in our entire collection: a travesty Last Supper "tapestry." I go for quotation marks because I don't know what else to call it—it's more like a really stiff, scratchy beach towel. And it's so poorly rendered that Jesus's forehead is twice the length of his hand (which prompts Jason to frequently quip, upon entering the kitchen, "Hey, Jesus, why the long face?"). Ray scales the "tapestry" Spider-Man-style and hangs there for a while, talons clinging to Judas's robe, contemplating her next move.

I contemplate mine as well. To attempt a grab would be foolish. I learned my lesson the first time I tried to pick her up and she used my palm as a pincushion. Should I fetch a broom maybe, and try to gently prod her off the wall and direct her toward the back door? Ray turns away from Judas and trains her good eye on me. It's as if she can read my mind and doesn't like the way the plot thickens. She lets go of the "tapestry," plunges into the bowl of bananas on the table, leaps off and races for the window, whereupon she begins hurling her small body against the pane again and again and again.

"Ray! Stop it, Ray!" I cry over her seemingly painful failures at defenestration. When she sees me near the window she takes off yet again, and I successfully block her from wedging herself behind the refrigerator, which leads her to jet down the hall again, thankfully toward the back door. I smack the handle to open it and out she goes.

Phew!

chapter 9

burial *at* curb

sunset park is home to

Brooklyn's own Chinatown. The commercial district lies on Eighth Avenue, sprawling through the 40s and 50s, and except for the lack of counterfeit Fendi, Prada, and the like it's on a par with Manhattan's Chinatown in terms of crowds, shops, and smells—some divine, some disturbing. I'm there at least once a week for vegetable exotica, to-die-for dumplings, and cheap seafood (tiger shrimp, $4.99 a pound!). Other marine life is also available, but I don't think it's technically "sea" and I personally wouldn't call it "food." Think stuff that begs the "pets or meat?" question immortalized in Michael Moore's *Roger & Me*. Buckets full of turtles, buckets full of frogs. Jason has so far been successful in discouraging me from purchasing a fat, slime-green frog as a third wheel for Iggy and Echo—he assures me that after some messy, torturous fun and games, Iggy and Echo would ultimately vote "meat!"

The side streets perpendicular and avenues parallel to Eighth are largely residential and largely Chinese. So when I first catch a glimpse of Mary, I profile her. I'm walking down the block, laden with tomato-colored sacks of bok choy and skinny eggplant, bitter, yellow-flowered broccoli, and leafy purplish cousins of the coleus (I don't know what they're called, but sautéed with enough garlic I don't care), and at first I don't notice her at all. I notice the cat. Solid gray—a "blue" in feline parlance—and utterly composed on the middle of a busy Saturday-afternoon sidewalk. I don't pss-pss-pss? him—I've got enough trouble—but cattraction nonetheless makes me stop and look.

He, however, only has eyes for her. And while his pace is an indolent meander—you know cats, they don't like to come off too eager—his trajectory is clear: He's headed for a short, compact woman in her sixties, with sharp black eyes and straight, blunt-cut hair more salt than pepper. Smiling, I approach her, and she smiles back—it's a *takes one to know one* smile—then returns her attention to the blue. She bows slightly, and the cat raises his nose to the extended fingertip of her liver-spotted hand.

"Boy," I say to her. "That one, I could be a three-hundred-pound wounded tuna limping down the street, he wouldn't know I was alive."

"Yeah, well, what can I tell you," she says modestly. For a Chinese lady, her accent sure rings of old-school Brooklyn Italian. And her black eyes are awfully round.

"You take care of him?" I ask.

"Him, sure." She tilts her head toward her driveway; I follow the tilt and think I spy someone furry scuttle along the wall. "Them out there. And the three in the house. But that's it, three in the house. You got to set limits."

Ah, a kindred spirit. I check out her house. Brick, two-family, somewhere between run-down and kept-up, calico sharing the bay window with a porcelain statuette that looks religious—a saint or somebody, the kind of thing you'd win at a Catholic carnival. "Yeah, I hear that," I say. "Very important to set limits."

After exchanging names, we banter a bit about the neighborhood. Mary has lived in Sunset many years—she is pre-Chinatown, and not at all Chinese. I wonder if she tries to pass—otherwise, what's with her quilted, frog-toggled, mandarin-collar jacket, part of the de rigueur ensemble of little old Chinese ladies everywhere? She says she doesn't mind the way the area has changed, that in the 1970s it was "the Wild West around here," that the Chinese are "a clean people." That's a huge compliment from a little old Italian lady. Trust Ashley on this. She's in real estate and currently has a listing for the house of a little old Italian lady, whom she has yet to see without a bucket and thick-bristled brush—scrubbing baseboards, ceilings, upholstery, rugs, whatever—with a solvent so strong it makes straight bleach seem as benign as chamomile tea.

From the corner of my eye I spy another streak of fur, and the conversation returns to felines. I tell Mary about my wards with the pride of a Texas rancher, then inquire as to how many head of feral she's got. Mary shrugs. "Hard to keep track," she says. "I try not to get too attached; don't even name them anymore. I just feed them—somebody's got to."

Now, I really do not want to insult this lady. As a general rule I respect my elders, and Mary represents my favorite species of senior, the tough old broad. I do not want to impose my views on her. She believes she's doing a good thing, the right thing—but I think, yeah, right, good for her. She acts all unsentimental but if it weren't for these driveway denizens, what—who—would she have? Is her husband alive? Do her children visit? Are there any other little old Italian ladies left in the vicinity for her to play canasta with? "So . . ." I cannot help myself. Mary feeds to breed. "You don't . . . fix them?"

"Huh?" says Mary. "Nah."

"Because, you know, there are vets all over Brooklyn who'll do it for a discount. There are these certificates you can get—like coupons . . . ?"

Mary is clearly not interested. "Yeah," she says. "Well . . ."

I tell her I'd better go, that it was nice meeting her. I put down my orange plastic sacks and go into my wallet for a twenty, which I try to press on Mary. She turns it down. "Not for you," I tell her, "for them . . ." Again she says no, thank you, and walks proudly up her driveway.

The blue, proudly, follows.

It's the first week of April and Jason and I will be making a road trip to South Carolina for his grandparents' golden wedding anniversary. I'm stoked—down there, I swear, it's pork at every meal. And down there is the only place you can get *mustard*-based barbecue—which, as I've been previously indoctrinated, beats the pants off your average *ketchup*-based barbecue. The whole town of Prosperity has been invited to commemorate Faye and Ardell Shealy's fifty years of wedded bliss, so it promises to be quite the shindig. (By the way—the name of the town? It's ironic. And I don't think intentionally so.) I have volunteered to "do something" and have been put on posy detail. I am given the phone number of the local florist and advised by Aunt Debbie not to talk to "any of the biddies" but to ask for Lyle by name—Lyle being, no doubt, the only out 'n' proud rainbow-flag-waver in all of rural SC.

The evening before the party, the immediate family sits down to a dinner of bacon-wrapped ham chops, which readies my belly for the party to come. It's a lovely time, unseasonably warm for early April. Mrs. Shealy looks smart in her peach suit and cotton-candy hair, Mr. Shealy snappy in plaid buttondown and what I believe are called "dress pants." The affair is a bit daunting for me, social retard that I am, but I do okay. Just about everyone there is either a Shealy or a Dennis, so if I call someone Mizz Shealy I have a fifty–fifty chance of being correct. I dole out punch and welcome folks at the sign-in registry book and eat more sausage balls than I care to count. A handful of folks do choose to choke-slam New York City ("We passed through it once on the way to Niagara Falls—oh, Niagara Falls is just beautiful!" is one of the more backhanded digs), but I manage not to "get my Brooklyn up." Perhaps pork products contain some sort of bio-chemical sedative, like the tryptophan in milk.

We're down there about a week, staying with Janelle and Mike, and let me tell you I don't miss the furbags one bit. They're in good hands with our house/cat sitter, Jason's friend Dave. I enjoy doing the dog thing with Millie the Lab and Betsey the mutt (a terrier-shepherd mix, with maybe some rottweiler thrown in). You call them, they come. You throw a soggy toy, they fetch the soggy toy. Extraordinary! Jason has fun with Millie and Betsey, too, but he is jonesing bad for the Igg Man. The ride home is a leisurely thrift-shop-stopping excursion through North Carolina and Virginia, and we actually find the coffee table and medicine cabinet we've been searching for, but on the last leg Jason's cat withdrawal gives him the jitters and he puts the pedal to the metal.

Dave reports that all the cats, indoor and out, were no trouble at all, yet mentions he thought we said there were four feral kittens. Uh, there were when we left. I burst into the yard for a homecoming head count. No one greets me at first, but then out saunters Paulie . . . and now Sid, now Nancy . . . and oh goody, Yeff Smeef. No Ray Snarls. No Ray for days.

When she shows up and mews at me weakly I hand-feed her some leftover chicken. Though she gobbles each smidgen I offer and doesn't appear feverish, something is off. I get a bad feeling about this. Still, I hardly imagine it will be the last I see of her.

The critter-catcher is in the mail. It should arrive in three to five business days. Yet despite intensive training from Neighbor-hood Cats—I am a card-carrying feral cat caretaker, they have sent me an actual business-card-type card attesting to this—I am sorely lacking in hands-on technique. I explain this on the phone to Jude from Muffin's when I call to order certificates (one male, one female, to start), and she tells me that if I like I can come to the Muffin's headquarters for a quick refresher course. I take her up on it, and call Jason to see if he'd like to meet me there.

I call him from my office; he is at home—he works a staggered schedule as a fact-checker at a popular music magazine, which al-lows him several days off in each two-week production period. The flexibility suits him, gives him time to do music. Today is a Vapours rehearsal, so I'm not surprised that he doesn't pick up the phone, rock bands being, by definition, rather loud. As it turns out, however, he and Rich and Ashley are out in the yard at the time of my call, taking a break and reveling in the balmy weather that followed us up from down south. No one wants to jinx it and say it really feels like spring, but no one's going to put on a jacket if no one really needs to. While they're outside, shooting the shit, taking the sun, luxuriating in the indie-rock lifestyle regular citizens can only covet, Ashley spies the flies.

Not a swarm, nothing that would inspire a Sci-Fi Channel movie, but more than a few flies darting in and out and around the cat house. "How come there are so many flies around the cat house, Jason?" Ashley asks.

Jason investigates. Then he calls me. The ferals haven't bothered with the cat house since the March thaw, but Ray must have figured it was a good place to die. He breaks the news gently, leaving out the part about the flies (later I learn from Ashley that it was she who played CSI). I begin to cry, softly, the way you cry when you're at work and the door to your office is open and you don't want anyone to hear because the last thing you want to do is explain why you're crying. Especially when the reason is a flea-bitten, half-blind, fully dead feral cat.

But it's not fair. Why Ray? Why not Yeff Smeef? Did he make her sick? Just another reason to hate him to the end of his entrails. Ray was my friend. That silly misunderstanding of her getting in the house and going berserk was water under the bridge. Ray was the first to take food from my hand. Ray was my partner in stick. Ray was going to become a charming little house cat someday. But she's dead and that's what ferals do, they die, better get with the program. They ought to call it trap-neuter-return-dispose. Speaking of which, Jason asks, between soothing "shhhs," what we should do with the body.

Damned if I know. We didn't bury my dearly departed cat Whoopie in the yard. The vet said it was illegal and carried a fine, and I dreaded some wild dog or displaced raccoon sniffing her out and digging her up. So we had her cremated, and her ashes now sit in a flowered tin on the bedroom mantel. Now I think that was dumb—we should have done the shoe-box-and-shovel routine, said a little eulogy, sat a little shivah. Whoopie only lived a few months in Sunset, but it was as much her house as ours. If we feared she would be fussy and pissy, hide in a closet for weeks, we were wrong. She sniffed the place from top to bottom, appraised and approved every inch, then made herself at home. And for the first time in years—since a brief August stint squatting in an LA duplex with no screens on the windows—she had outside access. Feeble as she was near the end, it wasn't like she'd be running off and getting lost. She'd simply hobble into the yard on arthritic legs to sunbathe and howl with senile gumption at bugs. Whoopie loved that yard, and should have been interred there. Who would know? Are space satellites bleeping over Brooklyn, taking photographs of illegal cat funerals?

Whatever—if my companion of twenty years didn't get a backyard burial, Ray the furbag wasn't getting one, either. I tell Jason to do with her what Matt and Amy do with their dead: Put her in a bag, walk her up to the avenue, and dump her in the trash can on the curb.

I'm not thinking clearly. I will come to regret not burying Ray, too. I will come to wish there was a little marker—a brick or piece of trashed picket fence—to signify Here Lies Ray Snarls, Feral and Friend.

At the moment, however, I just want it done. I don't want to see her. Indeed, I take the train directly to the Muffin's headquarters after work for my TNR tutelage. I don't know what I expect the Muffin's headquarters to be like—something akin to a hospital wing, or possibly the Pentagon?—but I guess I'm surprised that it's a one-bedroom apartment in a stately old Bay Ridge building. Jude herself answers the door, and I am immediately gob-smacked by her beauty. Her simple chignon is pure white, more silken than wispy, and her delicate, high-planed bone structure makes Princess Grace look like Mrs. Potato Head. Slender and erect, she wears her patterned, polyester blouse with an elegance I couldn't manage in head-to-toe Prada, and I assume she must have danced at some stage of her long life, probably *en pointe*. The only thing unattractive—but not uninteresting—about this woman is her mouth full of cockney teeth. She has a husband, or a man friend, or manservant, who is tall and stooped like Lurch but bald as Uncle Fester and must surely worship the ground beneath her feet; he seems to help her run the organization.

The apartment is tidy and virtually—remarkably—catless. I see only one, an aged longhair dozing on a kitchen chair, and don't catch a lingering whiff of feline, either. Jude bids me to enter the living room and as soon as I do I start snuffling again—I tell her about Ray. Jude does not exactly pooh-pooh me, she is sympathetic, but it's obvious this is not the first dead-cat story she has heard. Then Jason buzzes the apartment, and when I see him I blubber anew. Jude is charmed by Jason's southern intonation and "yes ma'ams"—most women are—and when she smiles at him, bad teeth notwithstanding, she is more beautiful than when she is not smiling.

Jude reminds us we are doing God's work, and shares a few anecdotes about human beings who for one reason or another cannot go through with TNR. She tells of people who think female cats enjoy mating, and that she must say in return: "What, do you think the males asked her out on a date? Plied her with catnip? The cat is being raped, possibly gang-raped!" Her most mind-boggling tale involves a lady who insisted the two cats she was keeping wouldn't breed because they were brother and sister. Jude shakes her silken white head. "And she was a registered nurse, this woman, if you can believe it!"

With that, Jude breaks out her trap.

"Watch," she says professorially. "It's one, two, three, four. Push, lift, pull, latch. Now you try."

Should be easy. Jude's trap even has bits of masking tape on its levers and latches marked 1, 2, 3, 4 to guide the novice cat-trapper. Okay, fine—easy for you maybe. I am not an especially nimble individual. I never met a lock I could open on the first at-tempt. USB ports puzzle me. It is a wonder, in fact, that I can tie my own shoelaces. So while Jason masters the contraption straight off, I struggle with it till I sense Jude's impatience, then promise to practice at home with our own trap. Following the les-son, Jude offers more wisdom. Concerning, for instance, bait.

"Cat food?" I venture, and when she doesn't blink, I add: "*Wet* cat food?"

"You can try," she says. "But most people report success with BumbleBee, solid white, in oil."

I should have brought a pad and pen to take notes, but I vow to splurge and go with the name brand. Next, Jude counsels me on being firm during the twenty-four-hour starvation period. Since I didn't feed this morning, all I have to do is survive the kittens' accu-satory stares this evening and I should be good to trap by morning. Jude reminds that if we don't catch a feral right away we must con-tinue to withhold food until we do. She talks about how some clever cats can get in the trap and eat the food without tripping the plate. How others will stick a paw into the cage and topple the tuna can. All this reiterates what I learned from the Neighborhood Cats seminar, and from Matt and Amy, and I'm beginning to fear cat trapping will be an existential nightmare worthy of dramatic exploration by Sartre.

When we get home I practice on the trap until I feel like a jar-head who can assemble and disassemble his M16 blindfolded. Still, I do not catch a wink, tossing and turning and fighting with the bedclothes all night. By morning sleep deprivation has denuded my ability to set the trap and the four simple steps take me a good twenty minutes. Finally, I get it locked; then I load—with BumbleBee, solid white, in oil. I stagger out into the yard and situate the trap amid the empty kibble bowls, then beat a hasty retreat to the back door. But before I can get inside, *slam!*

Gotcha! Whoa, this is too easy! I double back to see none other than Sid Vicious behind bars. And he's still fronting, still as a stone; he doesn't look pissed or even perplexed. I run into the house, make for the stairs to tell Jason, then remember the directive and ransack our linens for some towels crappy enough to sacrifice to the cause. To soothe the savage beast, the training goes, provide a comforting dimness.

Once outside again, I find Paul and Nancy sniffing and eyeing their caged sibling cautiously. "You're next," I mutter as I drape a towel around the ambulatory jail cell. My cat-trap manual has taught me to bring a caged feral into a quiet place as soon as possible. Makes sense—it would be tough to chill out with your brethren (or in this case, sistren) nosing about, going *nyah-nyah!* in catspeak. I intend to bring Sid into the bathroom, but lifting the cumbersome cage proves challenging, since the handle is now covered by crappy towels. Sid, thank goodness, doesn't thrash as I maneuver him into the house, turning in the narrow hallway to get inside the bathroom. I place the trap in the tub, then sit on the toilet and lift a corner of towel. Sid deserves an Academy Award for his phlegmatic performance, but I know he must be miserable. "Sorry, Sidney," I tell him.

Then I leave him alone and bound up the stairs, waking Jason with an exuberant yet gentle rattle to the shoulder. "Guess what? Guess what?"

"I can't imagine," he says drily.

"We got one!" I crow.

"Yeah?" He yawns, hugs his pillow. "Who?"

"Sid!"

Jason reaches toward the dresser for his glasses; I get them for him and place them on his face. "Okay," he says. "Now what?"

Ooh. Hmm. Er. Good question. I hadn't made specific arrangements, since I didn't think we'd snag a furbag so quickly. However, I had, upon Jude's recommendation, tried to get an "open appointment" with a Muffin's-affiliated vet. First I tried the doc who did Axl, but they wouldn't go for it, so I started down the list of veterinary practices till I found one that said I should just call as soon as I caught a cat and they would fit us in.

Of course, it is now only seven thirty in the morning, so I drink coffee and clock-watch. I leave a message at work, saying I won't be in today; I sneak a couple more peeks at Sid under the towel. After an hour I try the vet again and they tell me to bring Sid over. Okay, that would be my next stream to ford. How am I going to get him there? Sure, Mexicana Car Service was cool with Axl, but Axl was in a run-of-the-mill pet carrier, not a thirty-six-inch wire cage through which animal incontinence could pass onto the backseat of a Lincoln Town Car. I start flipping through my mental Rolodex for friends with cars. Rosemary often has access to the clownmobile, but she's on the Upper West Side of Manhattan. Gini and Dave are vehicular, too, but she doesn't drive and he has a "regular" job, meaning he has to be in the city by ten.

That leaves Ashley. Ashley's a Brooklynite, and she makes her own hours. Yes, Ashley would do quite nicely. Trouble is, I don't know her very well—I like her a lot, but we don't have history and she certainly doesn't "owe me one." Plus, I know her through Jason, and Jason doesn't like to ask for favors on principle. So before I ask *her*, I have to ask *him*. I get him out of bed, ply him with coffee, bring him into the bathroom to let him take a gander at the pathetic creature in the tub. Jason makes a scissor motion with his fingers and says softly to Sid, "Snippy, snippy, snip!" Of the ferals, Sid is his favorite—I'm hedging my bet with that when I mention calling Ashley. Jason's not nuts about the idea, but gives me his blessing.

"Heyyyy, Ashley, whatcha doin'?" I wheedle over the phone.

You really find out who your friends are when you've got ferals to fix.

Ashley has an SUV—a soccer-mom car, though Ash is more a gymnastics/skateboarding-camp mom, as neither Pearl nor Wyatt has expressed much interest in soccer yet. It's also a good car for schlepping band gear. We're about to see how it handles schlepping an unhappy feral. Ashley drives up and toots the horn; Jason and I are at the ready, lining her ample cargo space with a plastic tablecloth lest Sid have an accident.

Boy, do we feel badass, slinging into the Animal Clinic of Bay Ridge with our big towel-shrouded cage, cowing the pet owners with their pampered kittens in Sherpa bags and puny lap dogs in rhinestone-encrusted collars. It makes me feel like a bounty hunter, makes me want to haul my pants up over my belly and pound my fist on the counter. Then I flash on *The Elephant Man*: This morning, ladies and gentlemen, the part of John Merrick will be played by Sid Vicious.

A vet tech is summoned to bring Sidney down to the basement (a ripple of fear through me at the word *basement*, subduing my badassedness). A few hours later we return to pick him up, sans Ashley, Jason spreading the tablecloth on my lap in the backseat of the car service vehicle and placing the cage on top.

During his bathtub incarceration, Sid is a perfect—albeit melancholy—gentleman, or maybe more like a monk. He refuses food and water, and like it or not he's taken a vow of celibacy. The poor guy barely acknowledges us when we peek under the towels to see what condition his condition is in. I deliberate between holding him an extra day, just to ensure he's okay, and springing him after twenty-four hours. He seems so sad and listless I opt for the latter. We carry the cage out to the yard and, cue "Born Free," open the cage. Sid shoots out like a bronco, and I feel a great sense of accomplishment watching his tabby pattern disappear; I take Jason's hand, my smile of the bittersweet *our-little-one-is-leaving-the-nest* variety.

It doesn't take long before my sense of accomplishment begins to wane.

chapter 10

balls

this is the kind of morning

you wait for all winter. Warm, but not freaky warm, like those un-seasonable few days the first week of March that had Jason opti-mistically humping patio furniture up from the basement. That was "unseasonably" warm. Ironic adjective, *unseasonable*, if you live in the tristate area, though—weird weather is expected, prac-tically predictable. I have visited Central Park on New Year's Day with only a flimsy dungaree jacket for cover; I have slipped in slush on Easter, shivered at Fourth of July rooftop barbecues. This warm is bona fide—what your mother might call "warm enough." It's a warm you can trust. Spring, better late than never. And working stiff that I am, this Saturday morning marks my first opportunity to really get out there and enjoy it.

I can see spring, and feel it and smell it, when I hit the yard for the AM feeding. I see the yard with new eyes—spring eyes—and I'm in full revel mode. Despite the preponderance of dirt, no signs whatsoever of the lawn Jason sowed last year—not a patch, not a tuft, not a blade. He's been making noises about trying again, spreading seed, adding peat, throwing in some Miracle-Gro. Jason is a grass man. He hasn't said boo about flowers. Flowers are low priority. If we had a gardening to-do list, flowers would be penciled in somewhere on page 148.

The main problem with grass and flowers is Big Missy, mighty maple queen bitch, Jason's nemesis. She casts too much shade for anything delicate and sun-dependent to flourish. Right now Big Missy's dropping what we called polly-noses when I was little. Twin seedpods, joined at a seam and branching off into a straddle of green fins. I never knew what the *polly* part meant, but us kids would pick them off the ground, split the seeds apart with a thumbnail, and wear them on our noses—they'd stick, because inside the casing it's gooey. We had all sorts of names for things that fell off trees: fan tangos from mimosas; itchy-balls from . . . I can't remember what kind of trees those were. Oaks have acorns. Elms maybe? Whatever: itchy-ball trees.

Grass, flowers, yeah, that'd be nice—mostly I long for a lilac bush—but our backyard is possibly resistant to such suburban pleasantries. True, the Hinkleys have pretty shrubs scattered willy-nilly among their breeding lawn furniture; they'll bloom soon. But the Hinkleys have been on the block for decades; they've had opportunity for half-assed horticulture. Our house has been turned over numerous times in the last decade—"flipped" in real estate lingo. Big Missy is probably the only life-form intentionally planted in that dirt a century ago. Okay, maybe some hopeful soul installed the rose of Sharon back in the 1950s. But everything else is an accident, an immigrant, a stray. Ivy—roping, choking, sinuous snarls of it. Wild rose briar, heavy on thorns and sparse on petals. And weeds. Weeds, we got. Eternal. Tenacious. Tough weeds, pushy weeds, Brooklyn weeds. But they're green, they're alive—that's enough for me. I am celebrating Back-yard Appreciation Day, and the ivy, briar, and weeds help make this morning the kind of morning it is.

A Saturday morning, warm enough, and still early, so the only sounds are those found in nature. No reggaeton demand-ing: "Gimme that gas-o-leeeen-a." No car alarms, no traffic, no construction whirs from the post-fire site next door. Above, so far, no rumble of planes in the LaGuardia flight path. All I hear are birds, real birds, not pigeons. Chirps, cheeps, whistles, trills. The screech of blue jays (which, for the record, are awfully fond of cat food). The insignificant peep from a pair of cardinals I call Mr. and Mrs. DeBirdie (yes, it's apparently true that they mate for life—but their life expectancy is about a year). The rat-tat-tatting I took for an overzealous jackhammer the previous three morn-ings that I now realize is a woodpecker, an actual woodpecker. Big deal; after that linebacker raccoon on Super Bowl Sunday, I'm jaded.

Making coffee, I have Sid, Nancy, and Paulie in my sights. They've been romping and rolling since breakfast, crashing through ivy and abandoned lengths of corrugated garden fence, chasing squirrels up Big Missy. Raylene? Raylene who? They don't seem to miss her. *I* do. *I* miss Raylene. She was my friend. She played stick. This would have been a great morning for a friendly game of stick. But I can't go there, can't be maudlin. Kit-tens die. Get used to it. Think positive! This morning, this warm enough real spring morning, is my reward for our first successful TNR. (I consider it the first, as I did not trap Axl, I conned her). Sid is cavorting with his sisters, and I want in on the fun.

It's a little before eight and I am going to enjoy my coffee outside. Thunk of lock and squeak of storm door send the three stooges to greet me. God forbid I enter the yard without some treat for them, the spoiledest strays in Sunset. While I haven't transformed them into cuddly lap cats, the ferals do seem to have finally accepted me, not as a necessary evil but as a benevolent presence. Sure, they're still skittish—God forbid I sneeze in their vicinity, they scatter like I just shot off an M80—but that's cats, their fine-tuned senses combined with an innate skepticism. Even Iggy and Echo will look up from a doze with alarm if Jason or I make any sudden movements.

"What do you want from me?" I ask the ferals as I settle down with my coffee mug. "I just fed you."

It's nice living in a world that looks benignly on those of us who speak to members of other species. We're allowed to talk to animals. It's cute. Cuter than, say, talking to lampposts. Not that anyone can hear me, not to mention see me, this early on a Saturday morning. Throughout the winter my feral-slopping attire was largely concealed beneath a puffy down coat, but now it's spring and I must pay more attention to caretaker couture. Hence the outfit: orange suede Pumas and a matching velour caftan, vintage Halston III (total cost of ensemble: one dollar—the sneakers I scored from a wardrobe-stylist friend back in my LA days, the Halston a recent thrift-shop steal). I put my coffee on the table and pull up a chair. Paulie jumps on the opposite chair, then the table, to investigate the steaming mug. Now that Raylene is gone, Paulie's gotten noticeably bolder with me.

"Get your flea-bitten muzzle outta here," I tell her, swatting. I have to draw the line somewhere, and I draw it at sharing my coffee with a feral cat. I use my best gruff-and-grizzled character-actor voice—my Robert Loggia, my Van Heflin, my Lee Van Cleef, my Broderick Crawford.

Sid and Nancy ignore me and my coffee both, since neither of us smells like meat of any kind. They play. There are low-flying bugs about, and these backyard superheroes are out to rid the world of winged insects. They stalk, they leap; sometimes they go after the same bug and smack into each other midair. Very Wallenda Brothers, very Cirque du Soleil. Sid's really looking good for three days post-op; he's getting barrel-chested, growing into his big paws and Sphinx-like hooligan stare. In fact, he looks . . . wait a second . . .

Back to the house, into the fridge. Fling the tin foil off the leftover BumbleBee. Outside again, hunkered down like Jorge Posada, I'm very popular with all the kittens. But as I dole out greasy scraps of solid white, it's Sid I want to get up close and personal with. I try to position myself so I can feed and observe the cat's rear end and maintain my balance.

Why am I scrutinizing cat buttocks at 8 AM on a beautiful Saturday? Because, I could be wrong, but I'm thinking this cat is still working a total package.

Tuna makes kittens happy, and when kittens are happy their tails are perky. So as long as I am parceling out the BumbleBee, Sidney is obliging with his tail at attention; trouble is, his face (as well as Nancy's and Paul's) is in my face, not his hindquarters. So I yank gently on his tail to sorta-kinda swivel his haunches enough for a good look. Okay, are there balls there or are there not? Did I hallucinate these balls? Were these balls a trick of the lovely morning light? I have to know! The more I engage in gentle tail pulling, the more the truth is confirmed. I'm no authority, but those damn well look like cat balls to me.

That's when the phone starts ringing inside and, startled from my catcher's crouch, I topple over, spilling BumbleBee oil onto

Halston velour. It must be my mom. We usually chat Saturday mornings—but usually at nine, and usually I call her, so Jason can sleep. By the time I make it into the house, the phone has stopped and I'm glad because I don't want to chat—I think I saw cat nuts and am now on a mission. At the top of the stairs I find Jason, awake and disgruntled.

Not as disgruntled as I, however.

"Where's Iggy?" I rush past him at. "I need to find Iggy! I need to look at his ass . . ."

Jason is like: "Wha . . . ?"

"There he is!"

Iggy is languorously abed, sixteen pounds of indolent domesticity in fur pajamas.

"C'mere, Iggy!" I pounce.

Iggy likes to be chased. He may be a mattress walrus but he will move if he thinks you're going to follow him. It's one of his favorite games. But I am not playing. This is serious. "I am not fooling with you, Iggy!" His claws skitter on the hardwood. He's out of the bedroom, into the hall, the living room—phew, that's enough activity for fat boy. He hops onto a chair and I throw myself on him. I lift his tail.

It's neat as a buttonhole back there.

No sign of vestigial testicles whatsoever.

Jason is adjusting his glasses. His stretched-out boxers hang low. His cowlick sticks up. Comical, but who am I to talk, kneeling on the floor in tuna-stained Mrs. Roper attire, scrutinizing a cat's asshole. As to Iggy, he looks affronted, violated. Only Echo possesses any dignity at all. She strolls past on the way to the windowsill, eyes averted as if she doesn't know any of us and certainly doesn't want to.

"What . . . are you . . . *doing?*" Jason inquires.

"I'm upset," I say flatly.

Apparently, Jason doesn't say.

"I needed to check Iggy . . . I needed to see . . . I think something went wrong at the vet the other day."

"Huh?" Jason scratches himself. "What are you talking about?"

I stand up, look him in the eyes and utter one word: "Balls!" Then I bolt for the stairs. Sighing, Jason comes after me. "Sid!" I say, as if that explains everything. I search for the vet's number, the Muffin's number, somebody-anybody's number, in the TNR file I keep in the kitchen. "I was just out there, and I was . . . looking, okay, and it looks to me like that cat still has balls. I don't know, maybe they forgot to do him. He's just a feral, they have full-price paying patients. Sid's just some Medicaid cat, a charity case. I don't know, but I know what I saw . . . I think."

Jason doesn't say a word. Half a minute later I hear him buckling his belt. He's dressed. "Show me . . . "

Out we go. Jason's presence continues to arouse utmost suspicion among the ferals, but then again, I am with tuna. They take their chances; they swarm. Jason and I hunker. I make swipes for Sid's tail; he weaves, feints, dodges.

"Get him, get him!" Jason urges.

"I'm trying . . . there! Look!"

Sid escapes. "Damn it!"

"I can't see!"

"Here! Quick! Look!"

Jason gets a look. Then he stands, squints through the trees, shrugs. "Well, there's definitely *something* back there . . . ," he says finally.

Aha! So I'm not crazy!

The phone begins to ring, we run back to the house. It's Mom.

"Heyyyy—did you try to call a little while ago?" I ask.

"Yes, but I didn't leave a message—I didn't want to wake anyone."

"Is everything okay?"

"Yes—why? What's the matter?" She gloms onto the tension in my tone. There ought to be a game show, *Name That Mood.* My mom would be the reigning champ; she susses out my disposition in three words. Or maybe it's just the telepathy a mother has for her child: My mom's Ninar is in full blip. "Is everything okay there?"

"Yeah . . . but can I call you back in a little while? I need to call the vet. I think he might have made a mistake with one of the outside cats."

"A mistake? What kind of mistake? What do you mean mistake? How could he make a mistake?"

"Ma, I'll tell you later . . ." I hang up, locate the vet's number. No answer. No voice mail. I try Muffin's. Answering machine. What am I supposed to say: *So I took my feral to one of the vets on your list and they neglected to chop his balls off—just thought you'd want to know*? I can't do that.

Once I'm off the phone, Jason takes to the music room and turns on his computer to go online (we're still in the Dark Ages of dial-up). I can't imagine what, specifically, he Googles, but male cat neutering flicks onto the screen in livid color. We study it. We find another Web site dedicated to feline testicular removal. And another. We look at them all. Then we look at each other.

"I don't know . . . ," I say.

Jason goes offline and I try the vet again.

"Animal Hospital . . . "

"Oh! You're there!" I'm caught off guard. Now that someone's answered, I'm wondering how to phrase this.

"Can I help you?"

"Yes, um, I brought in a feral cat to be neutered the other day . . . and there's sort of, I think there's a problem."

"What kind of problem?"

"Well, I was just outside . . . looking . . . and it seems as though the cat still has testicles . . ."

"Excuse me?"

"Testicles. Balls." I feel myself getting on a roll, a jag, Tourette's-syndrome-style. "Nuts. Jewels. Bollocks. Oysters. Little kitty *cojones* . . ."

"Ma'am . . . ?"

"I'm sorry, I'm sorry, it's just . . . I mean, could it be the doctor forgot to do him? You know, you got busy, backed up? I'm just . . . I don't know if I'll be able to trap him again, and you guys took my Muffin's certificate . . ." I don't mention the extra twenty-four-dollar rabies shot and the fifteen bucks for antibiotics-in-a-dropper I'd sooner be able to administer to King Kong than Sid Vicious.

The receptionist asks my name and puts me on hold.

Jason sits at the kitchen table and yawns. I pour him coffee.

"Ms. Malkin?" she says. Behind her, dogs yelp hysterically. "Sid Vicious, right? Look, I've got his chart here—the doctor fills out the chart as soon as he's done with surgery, and everything seems to be in order . . ."

"Yeah, but . . . well, what am I seeing back there?" I know what she's thinking. She's thinking: Why am I *looking* back there? What kind of twisted sicko cat-pervert is she being forced to contend with?

"Well, sometimes it takes a while for the swelling to go down. It might even be a few weeks. At least it was with my dog . . ."

She's being nice, but I'm unconvinced. It's not that I don't trust her; I just know what I saw . . . I think. I'd like to speak with the doctor, frankly, but the part of me that is not inflamed and indignant about the whole affair is starting to feel like an idiot. I glance at the clock. It's nearly ten o'clock. Shit. I've got to get some clothes on, buy doughnut holes for my writers' workshop—I show up without sugar, those kids will lynch me. "Oh, okay, well, that clears up a lot," I fold. "But if it turns out . . ."

"You have your receipt, right? Just hang on to it and—well, I guess you could always bring him back. If necessary. But I wouldn't worry."

"Okay, well thank you. Sorry. Thank you very much . . ." She wouldn't worry. Nice for her.

chapter 11

ain't *no* stopping *us* now

the swelling of sidney's hind-
quarters markedly diminishes after about a week, and I'm convinced that his castration is complete. Flush with success, Jason
urges me to sally forth and TNR the two remaining kittens. I hear
him, but need a bit more recovery time for myself. Our slam-dunk
with Sidney notwithstanding, I found the ordeal fairly traumatic.
And who knows what he told his sisters? Bring out the trap too
soon and the forewarning will be at the front of their lima beans.
Besides, I'm not so sure nabbing The Sidney wasn't just a fluke.
This misgiving is validated at a party at Gini and Dave's.

Much to the dismay of their trio of indoor-outdoor cats—in
particular antisocial, asthmatic Frank, a wheezing geezer of a tabby
too frail to make it out of the bedroom these days, much less the
cat flap—Gini and Dave toss a throw-down once, sometimes twice

a year. Their stately Clinton Hill town house is conducive to friendly gatherings, with the wide, open spaces of its parlor floor and professionally landscaped backyard. (Tangent alert! Younger guests especially love that backyard, not so much for the landscaping but for Lucy and Elijah, Gini's two pet ducks; you know how little kids are about ducks. As to grown women and ducks, what can I tell you? Hailing from Wisconsin, Gini was raised by ophthalmologists, not farmers, yet she had a pet duck nonetheless and is perhaps going through a second childhood. Or maybe it's mere eccentricity, which runs deep in the Sikes clan. For instance, their dog named George, named George by Gini's father, Rex, who reasoned that if he was to be saddled with a dog's name, their dog ought be saddled with a human one. Anyhoo, Gini was devoted to her original duck until she poisoned the poor thing by feeding it chocolate cake. This was not premeditated murder—no fowl play involved—Gini was simply unaware at the time that chocolate is a duck-killer. Indeed, the bromine and caffeine—drugs classified as methylxanthines—in chocolate are toxic to most animals, and while death by chocolate is rare, you might want to keep Felix and Fido on a methylxanthine-free diet unless you enjoy cleaning up vomit.)

Back at the Gini-Dave shindig, Jason and I are having a good time, since Dave is an excellent cook and they know lots of nice smart people. Among them, the previously mentioned brilliant yet salt-of-the-earthy Sheri and Sean, who are frankly amazed at the ease with which we captured our first feral. I am amazed that they are amazed—like Jason, they are from the South, which I logically equate with all manner of huntin' and fishin' and wranglin'. Yet Sheri and Sean tell us that they've tried on numerous occasions to TNR their backyard squatters to no avail. I'm thinking: *You two were born below the Mason-Dixon line, you can banter blithely in Latin, but you can't catch a cat? Either you guys have been using a butterfly net, or Jason and I simply had beginners' luck.*

Musing on this, I wander off to stuff my face (food always helps when grappling with a conundrum) and fall into a conversation with another party guest. He's one of Gini and Dave's tenants, a handsome expat Brit who swears he's never met anyone in Brooklyn who was actually born here. This seems unlikely—people are born in Brooklyn every day!—but he's a nice enough chap and seems fascinated by me, and the rapt attention of a good-looking man is not to be dismissed lightly. "So do tell me, whatever was it like growing up here?" he inquires.

If only I had a rich, grisly reply, brimming with lurid details of gang initiations and rumbles under the Gowanus Expressway with which to regale him. I mention my *Saturday Night Fever*-esque adolescence, adding that I've never seen anyone eat pizza the way John Travolta does in the opening sequence (one slice atop the other), and that my high school was the first in the city—perhaps the nation—to install metal detectors. "I guess in the 'burbs, kids had all those bougie problems with cliques and popularity—you know, *Breakfast Club* fodder, *Pretty in Pink* shit," I say, amping my Flatbush brogue a bit for emphasis. "Me, I was just trying to avoid getting knifed." Of course, the closest I ever got to being knifed was an altercation with a hitter chick armed with a rattail comb. (We called the tough kids *hitters*, a 1970s update on *greasers*, and while I'm fuzzy on the etymology I presume we called them that because given the chance a hitter would hit you.)

This chat reignites my *Yo! I'm from Brooklyn—I can do anything!* mojo, so soon after the party I ring Rosemary to see if she can hijack the clownmobile and be on call as our feral ferry. I lock and load the trap again and—forewarned? forget about it!—some dumb furbag strolls right in. And goes berserk. Paul Wolke, Sunset's shrimpiest psychopath, bears no behavioral resemblance to the stoic, silent Sid. Indeed, her actions the first few moments in the cage would suggest she has the Tasmanian devil as a personal trainer. She screams bloody murder as I carry her into the bathtub-*cum*-waiting-room, and I hope she'll take it down a notch by the time Rosemary flips a U-ie at the bottom of our exit off the BQE. No such luck. Paulie is one vociferous she-devil as we ride to the Bay Ridge vet, and I'm relieved to drop her off. Whereupon Rosie and I commence to have a pleasant visit.

I make us chicken salad sandwiches, which we take into the backyard to lunch alfresco. Sid and Nancy sneak up and loiter around for manna from heaven, and I oblige, pulling chunks from my sandwich for their nibbling enjoyment.

"These cats have got it made," Rosemary observes.

I shrug. "Yeah, well, I live to serve."

"No, it's like your running a five-star feral hotel here, or you know what it is? Assisted living. Assisted living for cats."

Rosemary and I concur that old folks who balk at assisted living are out of their gourds; that we're ready for assisted living *right now*. Then she gets up to leave—she needs to get the van back to the clown by three—so I'm on my own for the return trip from the vet. When I come to fetch Paulie, the receptionist gives me a wearisome look and calls for the tech to "get the Malkin cage!" I wish she would add a heated *stat!* to the order—it would make this feel like some TV medical melodrama. But I am all for truth-in-memoir so, no, she does not add a heated *stat!* to the order. Besides, someone has fastened a hand-lettered CAUTION!!!

sign to the side of the cage, and surely CAUTION!!! carries the same heated impact as *stat!*

Not remotely groggy from the anesthesia, Paul is emitting violent, from-the-diaphragm yowls, but fortunately the car service driver isn't alarmed by the caterwauling—he has a crazy cat lady for a sister. It's not until we reach my block that he breaks a sweat.

"I don't think we should pull over here," he says at the sight of the hulking tattooed thugs assembled on a nearby stoop.

"You have to pull over here—I live here," I say. And think, Sunset-style: *And excuse you, I have a thirty-six-inch cage with a vicious animal inside; I'm supposed to walk from the corner? I don't think so!*

Despite the incident in which one of these local louts, besotted and spurned by a fickle Sixpack Sister, broke our upstairs door down, I've always told myself these guys were harmless. Didn't one of them, with the unlikely street name of Nacho (unlikely as his skin is black and he wears long dreadlocks—more appropriate would be Callalloo, or perhaps Beef Pattie), upon learning that Jason does music, chase us down the block one time to present us with his own self-produced CD? Wasn't that neighborly? Indeed, it was. Well, now's my chance to find out if these homies are not only harmless, but helpful.

"Don't worry, they're not bad guys," I tell the driver gaily.

"You sure, lady? 'Cause I've been held up . . ."

"Yes, yes, not a problem—they're fine," I promise.

Reluctantly, he idles by the curb and I bang on the window, gesturing the stoop-sitters for assistance. They trip over themselves to come to my aid.

"What you got in there?" one asks me.

"Nothing, nothing, just get it off me," I say, indicating the handle as I ease the towel-shrouded trap out the door. "It's just a cat."

Paul Wolke takes umbrage at being belittled and delivers a bloodcurdling shriek.

"That's a cat? Holy shit! Must be some tough cat!"

How right you are, oh astute juvenile delinquent. Especially when you consider that Paulie and her siblings, while not officially adults, have, at six months or so in age, reached full size. Paul is the smallest, but all our furbags are pretty puny in stature—well fed and healthy looking but from breastplate to tail hilt measuring about the length of your average remote control device. I've seen my fair share of ferals—delving into TNR has made me more acutely aware of street cats—and while I've observed some skinny, scrawny, sorry specimens, I've never seen any as diminutive as ours.

"Have you noticed how little the ferals are?" I ask Jason the following day. We are out in the yard; he has just finished seeding the dirt and is making a silent prayer to the Gods of Grass, I am there to lend wifely support—at least he's not digging an igloo. As if on cue Sidney, who'd been busy holding down a patch of sunlight along the back fence, gets up, stretches, circles, and returns to work. "I mean, compared with Iggy and Echo, or just about any cats I ever met, they're real pipsqueaks."

Jason nods. "Midgets."

I flash on Jenny, what highfalutin title she'd put atop their bogus pedigree papers. "Sunset Minis!" I crow. "We've got us some rare Sunset Minis up in here."

"Yep, the compact cat, the ideal companion for the animal-loving urbanite," he says. "Maybe we should breed them—export them to Japan."

I think of Paul Wolke in the bathtub, her stitches disintegrating as we speak, and Sidney, his formerly robust nut-sack diffused and shrunken to neutered dimensions, mere pignolis now, and give Jason a look. "A little late for *that*, don't you think?"

Since Paul is female, we keep her in solitary two full days. And you thought Wendy O. Williams was a hard case in *Reform School Girls*. Ha! I worry that once set free she will dedicate her life to tearing me to pieces, but as it turns out our relationship takes a decided turn for the better.

Symbols and sign language are crucial to interspecies communication, as you've no doubt noticed with your own animal friends. Perhaps your Pomeranian gets all excited when you collect your keys, or your goldfish puckers up at the top of the bowl when you pick up the canister of fish food. All I need do is pat my belly and Echo knows I need a snuggle in the breadbasket (whether or not she will fulfill this need is, naturally, up to her own discretion). All I need do is show Iggy a Chinese take-out container of garbanzo beans and he knows it's snack time. (Jason does not approve of giving house pets people food, as it only turns them into paunch-bellied lard-butt table-beggars, but he does concede to my doling out one garbanzo each per day, because not only does Iggy comprehend what a Chinese take-out container of garbanzo beans is, he does a squeaky little song-and-dance routine at the sight of the Chinese take-out container that Jason finds adorable.)

The outside cats, too, are coming to identify and understand certain visual clues. Most notably, Paul Wolkie identifies and understands that a wad of tinfoil means a treat of table scraps. (Jason has no objection to my using the ferals as a Flintstonian garbage disposal.)

Cats having excellent hearing, Paulie can hear the crinkle of tinfoil from three backyards away and, Pavlov-like, comes running.

When she sees the wad of foil she knows I'm going to bend over and fork over something good. Yeah, well, not today. Today I unfold the tinfoil and tilt it to give her a look and whiff of the contents (you know that weird purple-black meat on a swordfish steak no one wants to eat?), but I don't hand it over. This, as you might surmise, pisses Paulie off. Sid and Nancy have come around by now, but they hang back, as Paulie is going bonkers at my feet. She paces from one sneaker to the other, trying to determine what is *wrong* with me.

I taunt her, picking up a piece of fish, displaying it, and putting it back in the tinfoil. Paulie rises up on her haunches (the position, in cat yoga, known as Kangaroo Pose), whiskers twitching madly. Goes back to all fours, paces, mews indignation. Kangaroos, twitches, et cetera, ad infinitum.

"Ooh, swordfish!" I say. "Yum!"

Paulie is thinking, that lima bean in her cranium cranking overtime. She gives me a few swats to the leg, hoping a little physical intimidation will get me to deliver the goods.

"No dice, cat," I tell her. "You want fish, you're going to have to be proactive."

She sorts it out some more, calculating on her internal chalkboard a formula: Desire times fish divided by leap equals satisfaction. Then she makes her decision, tensing her entire remote-control-sized body for several endless seconds and jumping right onto my lap with the poise and precision of Nadia Comaneci.

"Oh, God, you're a genius," I tell her, extending her a chunk of fish flesh. She takes it in her mouth and leaps off my lap to demolish it. She repeats the lap-dance exercise over and over until half of the purple-black swordfish meat is gone. I feel kind of guilty making her expend so much energy when, with Sid and Nancy, I rip up what remains of the fish and lean over to offer it up. They approach, but Paulie, incensed, smacks them off. Fortunately I have two hands—Sid and Nancy take turns eating swordfish from my right while Paul pigs out from my left. Down now to the last little piece, I dangle it above my thighs.

"Who wants it?" I ask.

Paulie doesn't hesitate. My lap is now her exclusive domain.

So, symbols, right? We humans understand symbols, too; we respond to visual stimuli. The day after Paulie and I renegotiate the terms of tinfoil snacks, I go into the backyard to find something unusual strewn before the threshold. A string of alternating round and oblong wooden beads, some painted red, some yellow, some blue, which I trust to be the national colors of Ecuador, since attached to the string of beads, directly in the center, is a wooden amulet about the size of a silver dollar that reads ECUADOR in red, yellow, and blue letters.

Now, think what you will. Think the necklace arrived by gale-force wind gust. Think it was dropped accidentally by an errant Ecuadorian crop-duster. You are entitled to your explanation, as I am to mine. The necklace is a gift, and while I don't really go in for jewelry, it's a far more appropriate one than some half-eaten bird or slain mouse with rigor mortis. One of my Sunset Minis—Paulie, I'd wager—has brought me bling!

* * *

I have been neglecting Nancy. Sure, she gets as much kibble as the next cat, but in terms of attention she's gypped. She just doesn't interest me much. If I got her for a lab partner in high school chemistry, I would groan aloud. One of those skinny, dippy chicks with too much eye makeup. (Not that I didn't wear too much eye makeup in high school, a lot of it blue; I just wasn't skinny.) The kind of girl who wouldn't even notice I didn't like her because she was otherwise occupied basking in the kind of attention that matters—you know, male attention. I would be busy electrolyzing a potassium iodide solution and she'd be deciphering mash notes and getting her bra strap snapped from behind. This is not a far-fetched analogy. Nancy, with her ballerina neck and her moiré pattern and her Maybelline connection, is getting plenty of attention from the worst kind of male: Yeff Smeef.

I see this, because I have developed a sort of nervous tic—I cannot pass any of the back windows without going on feral patrol: I simply want to know who's out there, and what they're up to. And what I've been seeing—the villainous Yeff Smeef pursuing Nancy from yard to yard, his lecherous proboscis inches from her prepubescent coochie—distresses me to no end. I scold myself for playing favorites with the aggro Paulie and the chill Sid while leaving Nancy to defend herself against this prickle-dick menace. (Surely you know that the penis of a cat is covered with spines— if not, well, there's your trivia for the day; go ahead, impress your friends. The spines function as barbs during copulation, helping old tom hang in there. I've also read that this is the most erogenous area of the male cat, but quickly thought *says who?* and *ew!* and immediately stopped reading.)

Panged with guilt, I hurry out to the yard, vanquishing Yeff Smeef, who clearly despises me as much as I despise him. I make a great fuss about chasing him off, which of course scares Nancy away, too. But as I settle in at the patio table, a portion of my YA novel on my lap for pencil editing, she eventually comes around, as they all ultimately do, to see if I have anything tasty I want to get rid of.

"Ooh, hey, Nancy—come here, baby!" I coo, all co[n]
and amends-making. I curve my fingers in a come-hither ge[s]
but Nancy still shies away from my touch. She does, howeve[r]
figure-eight around the table legs to indicate she would certainly
accept a snack if I were so inclined. I don't happen to have any
meat on my person (going about one's daily business with meat
in one's pockets—just in case—is a sure and telling symptom of advanced feline mania, which I am glad to report I do *not* display),
nor do I have any choice leftovers in the fridge. So I trot inside
and hit the freezer to spoon her out an extra special treat of
vanilla ice cream, which I quietly, surreptitiously, place beside my
chair (quietly and surreptitiously in the hope that Paulie and Sid
won't catch wind and push Nancy off this most special of snacks).

And it is then, as I watch her joyously lick the daylights out
of Breyers Vanilla Bean, that I'm given cause to gasp. Nancy is
wounded, injured; she has been attacked—there are several
scabby scratches crisscrossing the length of her sweet, innocent
white snout to prove it. "That bastard!" I seethe, convicting Yeff
Smeef on the spot. What, you think some other cat's claws responsible—those of her wicked half sister Paul, perhaps? No, Nancy is
a special vic, of this I am sure to the depths of my guts. And I feel
awful about it. There's nothing I can do to alleviate the
scratches—chasing Nancy around the yard with a gooey dollop of
bacitracin on my finger would no doubt prove futile. Plus, I'm
equally helpless to prevent her from future run-ins with that
Aqualungian letch. My mind races, as it inevitably does, to the
gamut of awful things that could befall my ferals, from infections
to sexual abuse, and my inability to ease their pain and suffering in
any way. I want to scoop Nancy up and get her prompt medical

ant to punt Yeff Smeef all the way to Benson-
cement overshoes and drop him unceremoni-
nus Canal, but I can't do that, either.
hisper. "Poor baby."
few days later that the realities of backyard
d in an even more horrible way.

A best friend, when you're a little girl, is someone you see every day. A best friend when you're a teenager is someone you see every day and talk to every night on the phone. A best friend when you're a young woman is someone you talk to every day and get loaded with every weekend. But a best friend, when you're a homeowning, husband-having, grown-up woman is someone you e-mail often and call less often and see less often than that, even though you love her as much as ever. And, as we aged, Gini and I both developed a telephone aversion—while we once gabbed endlessly we now rarely ring each other unless absolutely necessary. Mostly—when amused, when irritated, when needing advice or hungry for malicious gossip—we rely on e-mail, and we know each other so well we don't have to resort to "cute" little :)s or ;)s or :(s to get our emotional import across.

So when I e-mail Gini to complain about what an asshole someone or other has been and she doesn't reply with quick, unconditional commiseration, I get a weird-bad feeling and pick up the phone. She doesn't answer, and I leave a message. Finally, a few days later, still too overcome to speak, she e-mails me to describe what she discovered upon going out to feed her ducks: Lucy dead, her head missing, her throat a bloody stump, and Elijah, barely alive, looking like he had done battle with a *T. rex*.

Elijah was whisked off to the Animal Medical Center in Manhattan, and subsequently to a waterfowl sanctuary in Connecticut, where he is expected to make a full recovery. Gini, I think, never will—since how can she achieve closure? One surgeon looked at the wounds and pronounced pit bull. Another vet surmised that because Lucy and Elijah had been in their pen at the time of the assault, only a cunning and dexterous animal could have worked the latch and gained access—he blames a raccoon. Whoever was the culprit, it's devastating to see survival of the fittest play out savagely in your own twenty-by-twenty patch of Eden. We fool ourselves into thinking we can protect the ones we love—our children, our mate, our animals—until forced to realize how truly ineffectual we are.

I think of the three cats I have fed and lost over the last few months. I think of the recent shooting a block away from us—gang-related, drug-related, the victim a seventeen-year-old boy. I think of the crazy stuff I did as a kid—driving on angel dust, swimming on quaaludes—and how I managed to slip through the Reaper's radar. And whenever anyone dies senselessly, I think of my dad. One day everything's great—he's mowing the lawn at my parents' post-Brooklyn abode in Oceanside, Long Island; he's hitting the yard sales with my mom; he's riding the little fold-up bike he keeps in the trunk of his Honda should the urge for a bike ride come upon him. The next day, bam, whump, God says "C'mere, Ted!" and he's dead of a heart attack. Just like suddenly, senselessly that.

Then I think of Mark, a British feral with an extremely hardy immune system, who lived to the ripe old age of twenty-six (if you believe Wikipedia). I think about what I can do for the life and well-being of the ferals I've taken on, conclude it isn't very much, and resolve more firmly to do it anyway.

I can starve—and starve I will. I can trap—and trap I will. And if all goes well, in a few days I can and will return triumphant. Because if I get Nancy spayed, she'll lose her allure and Yeff Smeef will leave her alone.

Trouble is, with TNR, there's no way to guarantee that the cat you want to snatch will be the one who winds up in the cage.

chapter 12

making plans *for* nigel

on feral patrol from the bedroom window, I notice Nancy sitting by herself in front of Stonehenge. Stonehenge is the three irregular slabs of white marble Jason found in the yard and used to create a bench, in homage less to the actual megalithic ruin than the midget version immortalized in *This Is Spinal Tap*. What's odd is that, even from my upstairs perspective, Nancy seems to have doubled in size overnight. Surely my love is powerful, but that powerful?

I head down to investigate further, but just as I open the back door, Paul Wolke—undaunted by her sister's apparent steroid use—marches up to the newly enlarged Nancy and pops her one right on the nose. Ever since Paulie began jumping on my lap, she has come to treat me the way a pasha treats a prized odalisque: as property. I am now officially hers, and she will brook no touchy-feely fraternizing between me and the other ferals. When I pet Sid, or try to pet Nancy, she goes into attack mode—and has developed an MO that would suggest she's viewed footage of the Gestapo: She storms her objective, and at approximately two inches from his or her face rears onto her hindquarters while still managing a forward, frighteningly goose-step-like projectile motion, then administers what I believe is known in boxing vernacular as the one-two-one punch, a left-right-left claws-bared series of swipes to the kisser. How special does this make me feel? Very. It's as close as I shall ever come to having two boys fight over me.

Still, I wouldn't want Paulie's affection to deter my budding relationship with Nancy. Nancy, however, is easily bullied to the sidelines—which is when I realize that this supersized Nancy is not Nancy at all. Because here comes the real Nancy, harassed by Yeff Smeef—who stops short of our yard to hunker in all his impressive repugnance beneath a Hinkley chaise lounge.

"So if you're Nancy," I say to the real Nancy, "who's . . ."

I scan the territory to make sure I'm not having an acid flashback complete with double-vision hallucination. Just then, in a streak of filthy white, Yeff Smeef darts out and lunges toward the Nancy impostor, chasing non-Nancy off more effectively than Paulie did. (The May–December romance he is pursuing has clearly put some pep in Smeef's step—either that, or he has the hookup for kitty Viagra.)

Non-Nancy is banished . . . momentarily.

This being a beautiful Sunday and me having nothing else to do but cat-watch, I keep on peep for the newcomer. Idly I wonder why the "vacuum effect" a colony of cats is supposed to create—that invisible scent fence to discourage outsiders—doesn't seem to be effectively vacuuming in my backyard. I wait until Sid and Nancy and Paul mosey off to unseen sections of the territory. I wait less patiently for Yeff Smeef to come and go as well.

And then I venture to entice. It takes a few pss-pss-psses to get some action, and the way the cat responds you'd think someone installed one of those invisible electric fences while I was asleep. The cat hunches forward, hesitates, then lurches back as if shocked.

What the hell—I've got all day! "Pss-pss-pss?" By verbally beckoning this stranger, whom the other ferals clearly do not want around, I laugh in the face of nature—never a good idea. Nature says: This is cat business; please don't meddle. Nature says: Haven't you got a novel to finish? Nature says: Remember the Parkay commercials of your youth in which Nature got annoyed when the margarine masqueraded as butter—annoyed to the accompaniment of serious thunder and lightning? But I can't help myself; cattraction is a powerful force.

I throw in a few of those smooching construction-worker noises, too. After all, don't I *need* to see this cat, so I can discern the difference between this cat and Nancy, my new best feral? Plus, come on, you got to root for moxie—this must be one tough nut to try muscling in on Sunset Mini turf. Slowly the cat encroaches. Very slowly. I'm like: *Damn, cat—I may have an open agenda but I've also had two cups of coffee this morning and need to pee like the proverbial racehorse.*

The aroma of fresh kibble finally does its magic, and the newcomer crouches bowlside and crunches away, glancing up at me nervously every few bites. I examine the specimen with scientific detachment; if I had a beard I'd be stroking it. Yes, similar face to Nancy, tabby markings on the forehead parting in a reverse widow's peak to reveal a scratched white snout, pink nose, and heavy kohl eyeliner. But this cat's eyeliner extends on one side into a teardrop tattoo. And his lower lip is black, lending a Goth effect. Plus, while Nancy's coat, like Sid's, has a moiré pattern, this tabby is dappled, with a tail striped as a barber pole. Then there's

the size factor–the beast has a few ounces and inches on Nancy–
and he lacks her long, elegant neck. But the greatest difference, I
note, as the cat finishes eating and bounds off, is that he is clumsily bowlegged, and most definitely a he.

Now, now, now: No need to be hasty. No need to tell Jason that
we've got another feral mouth to feed. This cat could simply be
passing through. And judging from the greeting he received from
Paul Wolke and Yeff Smeef–more Panzer tank than welcome
wagon–they're set to ensure he's passing through. Besides, even
if he hung around for a couple of days, Jason would probably just
confuse him with Nancy anyway; on a quick take they really do
look remarkably alike.

If he even exists at all. I'm not saying he's my imaginary
friend, the feline equivalent of the Púca, but his presence makes
no sense. Where did he come from? How did he suddenly mani-
fest in our backyard? It's as if his molecules coalesced out of dirt
and weeds, or he was beamed down from the *Enterprise* by
Scotty. Is he related to our original feral family–"blood kin" as
Jason's great-grandmother would say? Not that it would endear
him to Paul Wolke any. I've come to the conclusion that despite
my return day in and day out, the ferals consider kibble to be a
nonrenewable resource that could run out at any moment. Hence,
trespassers–be they country cousins or emissaries sent by Captain Kirk himself–will not be tolerated. Chances are, I won't be
seeing hide nor hair of this new cat tomorrow.

As it should be. So how come I can't even wait till Jason finishes his first cup of coffee before busting out with: "I think we
have a new cat!"

"No," he says.

It's a normal reaction. No normal person wants a never-ending stream of ferals in his backyard. Normal people want to cultivate grass, not cats.

But then he says: "Where?"

Atta boy! Curiosity kicks in. He takes his coffee and follows me outside, but of course the newcomer is not within visual range. Perhaps he already has passed through.

"Well, he was here this morning," I say. "He ate . . ."

Jason regards me the way the kindly but beleaguered asylum attendant regards the loony but benign paper-slippered patient and strolls over to inspect his grass, flora replacing fauna in his attention span. "Look!" he says proudly. "I think we're getting some tufts over here. I should water . . ."

The Vapours have a gig Sunday at Otto's Shrunken Head, a tiny tiki bar in the East Village, and I decide to go. To ease the angst of pre-trap starvation, it's best if you're not around to witness a bunch of cats working their best Bil Keane impressions at the kitchen window. The band before the Vapours seems to have about fourteen people in it. The bass player straps on a five-string. One of the female singers is wearing a skirt made (by her own two hands, I assume) from stitched-together men's ties. Neither the five-string nor the tie-skirt bode well—not to mention the mass quantities of personnel—and as I suspect, the band is kind of "jammy" (i.e., irritating). What's more, they have the temerity to play a pair of Beatles covers (if you're going to cover the Beatles, you'd better not butcher them).

Then the guy who books the club—a Brillo-haired, white-Russian-swilling older man (read: older than me) who very much resembles *Gong Show*–era Chuck Barris, brings on the Vapours. A three-piece with three songwriters and three singers means at the very least a variety of tunes. Ashley's got a new one about a plastic cup, called "Plastic Cup," and her shy, atonal vocals make Cat Power sound like Mariah Carey. Rich's rendition of "I Disappear" is a sexy, stream-of-consciousness showstopper. And Jason? What can I say? His western shirt and big red Epiphone, his floppy hair, and the way he pushes his round wire glasses up the bridge of his nose between chorus and verse lend him an aw-shucks rock god vibe that's irresistible. Tonight they do "Cow Song," a normally peppy country number, Valium-style, and they toss in their version of the Ramones' "I Love Her So." Everybody screws up at least once, and nobody seems to mind.

Nice set! But I quickly kiss Jason good night and bid Ashley and Rich adieu before slinking off in a taxicab. I have to get up early tomorrow—a trapping day. I'd pre-arranged with my last friend-with-car (Gini's Dave) to give me a lift to the vet in the AM if I do in fact nab the Nanster.

I haul out the towel-draped cage and slide in a particularly smelly can of tuna. (Due to household economizing efforts I saved thirty cents by purchasing, instead of reliable BumbleBee, the White Rose brand, and must now fret about the appeal of generic tuna.) Paulie leaps onto the top of the cage and rolls around on her back; she seems to have acquired a strange attraction to the towels. Sid and Nancy sniff around warily, while my nemesis Yeff Smeef skulks the perimeter. I heave a sigh. As I was taught in the Neighborhood Cats seminar, this is a problem with the one-cat-at-a-time approach to trapping: a previously TNR'd cat could enter the cage while the ones still in full possession of their reproductive organs steer clear. Okay, this might take a while. I go inside to brew coffee.

Twenty minutes later I lift the towel to find—yuck! blech! ugh! gak! pooey!—Yeff Smeef in the cage. Indecision renders me a statue. I don't want to waste a valuable Muffin's certificate on this diseased animal. I don't want my house befouled by this diseased animal, no matter how briefly. But if I take this diseased animal to the vet, might he not encourage me to do the humane and merciful thing and recommend the popular euphemism for euthanasia: put him to sleep? Of course, I don't have a discount death coupon and would have to go totally out of pocket, but Yeff Smeef would be gone, gone, gone from my life forever—a bargain at any price.

It's hard to look at him, even more malignant and malevolent behind bars. His fetid fur, his off-white eyes, his aura of consummate evil—he's a twisted Nick Cave lyric waiting to be written. I deliberate, agonized, a few moments more, the other ferals watching idly as if they'd made penny-ante bets. Then I decide. I opt for irrational. I slide up the guillotine side of the cage and hiss, "Get lost, Smeef!"

Yeff Smeef bolts.

I reset the trap and head upstairs to dress.

Jason and I are both ready to catch the train to our respective places of employment when we go out the backyard for a final trap check. And lo and behold if it isn't Nancy cowering forlornly in the corner! Oh . . . it's not . . .

"That's not Nancy?" Jason asks.

"No," I say. "It's the new one, remember, I was telling you about?"

"Are you sure?"

Yes, damn it, I'm sure. This cat is dappled, not moiré. This cat has black lip liner and a teardrop tattoo. This cat is twice the size of Nancy and has testicles. Doesn't Jason know *anything*? "Yeah, I'm sure," I say. "What should we do?"

"What do you mean, what should we do?"

"Well, Yeff Smeef was in here earlier and I let him go."

"You let him go? Why'd you let him go?"

"Because . . . I don't know, I let him go." Jason considers my fear of Yeff Smeef about as rational as my fear of basements and brain tumors, but doesn't chastise me for springing Yeff Smeef, as we have more urgent matters at hand. "So . . . what about this one?" I ask.

Jason looks at the trapped cat again. "You're sure it's not Nancy?"

"Positive."

"Well, I say, you step in the cage, you pay the consequences," he says definitively. "Whoever you are."

That is how Nigel Tufnel, named for our favorite *Spinal Tap* character, becomes part of our feral family. His position? Whipping boy. Try as he might to join the rumble-tumble games of Sid, Nancy, and Paul, he is thwacked off as a nuisance time and time again. But he's not budging. He plays with himself—he chases his tail. If you have never seen a full-sized cat do this you are missing something major. When kittens do it, it's cute. When adults do it, it's fall-down-gasping-for-air hilarious. Nigel Tufnel chases his tail the way David Mamet writes dialogue, the way Chet Atkins finger-picks, the way Paris Hilton parties. Nigel is a champion tail-chaser. Still, he is so lonely.

Loser!

Any wonder why I fall so hard and fast in love with him? It becomes not merely my desire but my duty to pet him, and it proves easy enough because he is so damn desperate for camaraderie. I extend curled fingers; he is there for a sniff. I sneak up to place my palm ever so gently on his back when his head is in the kibble and he flinches as if struck, but doesn't run off. Soon I am able to scratch his coccyx, sending his ringed tail straight into aerial position, stroke his back, and rub him between the ears. Only problem is, Nigel is a tad schizo. He'll be loving my caress and then, for no apparent reason, flatten his ears and smack my hand.

The casual observer would assume Nigel is simply high-fiving me, but the casual observer does not feel my pain. Sometimes Nigel's smack results in a scratch, but more often than not one of his claws sticks to the meaty part below my thumb or the delicate area between thumb and index finger—you know, the place you believed as a kid you should never get cut, as that could lead to lock-jaw (and might still believe, if you happen to be me). Yet when Nigel's claw submerges deep into my fleshy part, we are joined, he and I, for a second or two, and our eyes meet, shock and anger in them, that look you and your mate exchange in the heat of a quarrel when one says something sadistically below the belt and you cannot tell which one is more shocked and angry, the target or the shooter.

Neither one of us can bear to pull away, so we are still. Eventually his claw will ease out of its own accord. Nigel will then arch his back and rub against my shin as though nothing happened. And I will let him get away with it. Codependent much? With one hand I reach down and pet him, while watching a bright spot of blood bloom on the other.

"Why'd you do that, Nigel?" I whisper. It is meant to scold; it is meant to soothe. "That's not very nice . . ."

Then I bring the hole in my hand up to my mouth and suck the blood.

chapter 13

to purr *is* feline

"call your lawyer," rosemary

says with a snicker. "I think you've got a lawsuit here, babe."

Rosemary is not on her way to a gig, she doesn't even have the clownmobile. Having traveled via subway from Manhattan's Upper West Side to give me a present—the Crazy Cat Lady Action Figure by Accoutrements, Outfitters of Popular Culture—she can now take pleasure watching my face as I realize how much the Action Figure resembles me: frizzy blond hair (well, as frizzy as plastic can approximate), wide-eyed stare, flannel pajama couture.

Very funny, Rosemary. What's not funny? After we nab Nancy, there'll be no more cats to fix. Performing TNR on Nancy, the final feral on our to-fix list, will mark the end of our foray into wild cat hell (sorry, but Yeff Smeef doesn't count). It's a denouement I anticipate with some bittersweet sentiment. Why bittersweet? Why not total bliss and outright, washing-my-hands-of-this-messy-affair relief? Because reluctantly or not I can cop to it: My name is Nina, and I'm from Sunset, and I'm a crazy cat lady.

However will I spend my days? Macramé?

Still, I'm not about to leave Nancy prey to that would-be cradle-robber Smeef. So Jason and I plot her capture. And it takes plotting! While I may characterize Nancy as a ditz, I fear I've been unfair—after all, she has so far been wily enough to elude the trap. How, then, will we snag her? Better bait—kitty caviar, anyone? Perhaps a trickle of catnip on the trip pedal? It occurs to me then that our poor, deprived, underprivileged ferals have never even tasted catnip, and I promptly fill a lone sock with wacky weed. (What, you don't retain single socks for this very purpose, not to mention the myriad other uses for single socks, such as . . . well, I'd give you the litany but I think I may have used up my tangent quotient already.)

Outside in the yard, Sidney saunters up. I toss the loaded, knotted sock in his direction. He runs for cover as if I'd lobbed a live grenade his way, but cautiously makes a circuitous reapproach and takes a sniff. Giving a cat catnip for the first time is comparable to introducing some younger kid on the block to the joys of marijuana, like you did when you were a munificent high school junior with half an ounce of Panama Red. Only more fun, because humorous as the newly stoned younger kid might have been, he or she did not writhe deliriously around on his or her back, kicking a single sock in the air with his or her thumpers. (If he or she did, you were being generous with your Maui Wowie, and I got to admit I was never that generous.) Besides, you can be completely without guilt turning cats on to catnip because catnip is not a gateway drug. If you're a cat looking to get high, catnip is pretty much it.

Soon the nip-sock is sampled by the other ferals, and they all concur *Nepeta cataria* is a beautiful thing. Nigel nuzzles up and is sent into a whirling tarantella of tail-chasing frenzy. Even Yeff Smeef gets a snootful and lies dazed and disgusting in the sun. The sock is last seen being carried (okay, dragged) off to parts unknown in the mouth of Paul Wolke. So I've learned our outside critters like catnip (more than a third of felines take a whiff and go "feh!"). That doesn't mean a liberal sprinkle will inveigle Nancy into the trap. If anything, it will entice all the ferals to converge within. Talk about a slam-dunk winning entry for *America's Bloodiest Home Videos!*

Jason tells me I'm overthinking. He's always smirked in regard to my allegiance to BumbleBee solid white in oil, and an *I told you so* was no doubt on the tip of his tongue when generic White Rose brand lured both Yeff Smeef and Nigel Tufnel into the cage. I don't answer back snippily—just in case he's, you know, *right*—but head to the office musing on the imminent mutant spawn of an unholy alliance between Yeff Smeef and Nancy Vicious. Meanwhile Jason's toil for the day will involve refinishing the old-school medicine cabinet we picked up along with our disco coke table on the way back from South Carolina. He sets up a workstation out in the yard between two sawhorses and gets down to sanding off the rough surfaces.

Around four in the afternoon he gets company. Nancy has decided to check his progress. She sits daintily a few feet away, licking a paw in the shade and appraising Jason's sweat.

Jason says, "Hey, Nancy."

Nancy says nothing.

Funny, though they were vociferous hissers when they were small, none of the ferals is growing up to be a big talker. Paulie's yowls when taken into custody amount to the beginning and end of their articulation. It's occurred to me that this might have something to do with life in the great outdoors, since Iggy and Echo, who live in the great indoors, vocalize like Joan and Melissa at the Golden Globes. Sure, I chat up the ferals when I'm in their presence, but Iggy and Echo are veritably bombarded with conversation, song lyrics, television dialogue, and let's not forget the screaming diatribes from the Sixpack Sisters upstairs. This is why, I surmise, Iggy and Echo have such advanced verbal skills—mepp, prow, wee-mray, ming, whiff, all examples of their elocution—whereas the ferals are fiercely tight-lipped. I actually sort of miss the hissing and spitting of their kittenhood, but since they gave that up they've never so much as meowed.

Not to mention purr. As far as I know, purring as a concept is completely foreign to them. Sid and Nancy and Paul and Nigel have no idea what it is to rumble with pleasure. What a waste. I've often wished I had a little inner engine I could kick-start to show contentment, to say, without saying, things like *Yes, that feels nice, please continue* and *Ghirardelli—mmmmm!* Each of the furbags is equipped with a purr mechanism—they just never had a reason to use it.

So Jason says again: "Hey, Nancy," and Nancy sits there. All by herself. No other cats. Jason decides to get the cage. Now, if I were home, I would have had no choice but to get all Daffy Duck on his ass, crying, "No, no, no! You're going about this all wrong!" Consider: There had been no twenty-four-hour starvation period. There isn't tuna of any kind in the house. Futhermore, Jason sets up the trap, then goes back inside for bait, when my MO has always been to place the trap in the yard fully loaded. Men! Ugh! Can't they do anything right?

Off he goes to forage in the pantry. Something in an anchovy perhaps? A slab of SPAM? A can of salmon? Nope, our cupboard is bare of such smelly delights. What about the fridge? He begins to forage for appropriately rank leftovers, but must have finished them for lunch. Hmm, there's this ham. Whenever Jason's grand-folks send a care package—for a holiday, or one of our birthdays—there is always, amid the addictive seven-layer bars, Chex Mix, and occasion-appropriate greeting card, some sort of shrink-wrapped bright pink cured-pork product. Who knew you could mail meat? This freaks me out, and I immediately put any parcel-posted pork in the refrigerator, as if the cold could work some retroactive anti-trichinosis magic. Of course it's out of the question that Jason would waste this as-yet-unopened ham specimen on a furbag, which means all he's got at his disposal is kibble. Kibble! Hah! What kind of bait is that?

The unnecessary kind, as it turns out. When Jason returns to the yard, there's no Nancy in sight. At first he assumes she's wan-dered off and he missed his chance, but whom does he find abashed beneath the curtain of ninety-nine-cent-store towels? The little dolt just blundered on in. Jason stows her in the bath-tub and calls me at work to gloat, then jokes about putting an ad up on Craigslist, pimping us as the husband-and-wife cat-catching team par excellence: "Got ferals? Never fear! Nina and Jason are here!"

I hang up vaguely dismayed and go online to suss out a pet store in Manhattan where I can conveniently buy a Muffin's cer-tificate. The next day we're so blasé about our latest snatch, we don't even bother to pester a friend-with-car. Without telling the dispatcher from Mexicana that I'll be having feral on board, he sends the fleet's only hatchback and I sling Nancy inside. Animal clinic personnel greet me with jocular *here-she-comes-again* famil-iarity. I really am getting good at this. Too bad I'm done.

Almost. Going through my feral file I'm reminded that the ASPCA operates a "spay van" that roves the five boroughs neutering furbags for free. So even though our two females, Paul and Nancy, have been rendered impregnable, and despite my profound and abiding hatred for him, I make an appointment to take Yeff Smeef to the mobile castration unit, coming next month to a Brooklyn neighborhood near me. How soon? Soon enough, in two weeks, on the cusp of the Memorial Day weekend. Jitney out to the Hamptons, dahling? Back-to-nature camping trip upstate? Nah, no thanks—I'd rather babysit a fetid feral in my bathtub. Of course, maybe I'll get lucky—maybe the spay van vet will take one horrified look at Yeff Smeef, term him terminal, and advise me to do the "humane thing."

Throughout the ensuing weeks I do endure the predicted mixed emotions in regard to the rest of the furbag batch. Nancy and I have grown closer since her hysterectomy. She even lets me pet her now, and I take great satisfaction out of being able to cop a furry feel off this most skittish of ferals.

Speaking of copping feels, Nigel has become less prone to the snap-and-slap when I administer affection. To the tight-knit trio of siblings he's still the odd man out, the uninvited guest who wouldn't leave, the embargoed barger-inner, Rudolph without the Christmas-saving schnozz. But to me he's a puddle of need in a spotted coat. I recognize his neediness as I recognize my own, and I give him credit for not fronting (the way I do), for not pretending he does not need. Because I befriended him with relative ease, I wonder if he ever had a home, ever sat on a lap or nestled in an arm crook or slept on a bed, the lump between two lovers. I wonder if his now waning tendency to attack without warning is a symptom of former abuse—at the evil whim of some idiot adult or undisciplined child I would gladly throttle given the chance. He is better off cast out than used as a soccer ball. He is better off here, in the backyard jungle. Alone, but not completely. Nigel, sometimes, he's with me.

And as spring segues into summer Sid Vicious begins to range less, stick closer to home. Every morning, on feral patrol from the upstairs bathroom window, I spy him in his favorite new spot on the roof of the cat house, paws tucked under his chest and tail wrapped close alongside his body, head tilted down contemplatively. (In cat yoga this is known interchangeably as Brooding Hen Pose and Meat Loaf Pose.) There's something reassuring about seeing him there, so composed, so serene. Sid exudes an every-little-thing-going-to-be-all-rightness, a be-here-nowness, that I can appreciate only in moments like these, by myself on the toilet.

Perhaps I was wrong to read Sid as distrustful and standoffish during his kittenhood; perhaps he simply always had this gentle reserve, this ability to just be. How wistful it makes me—I can never just be, am always tussling with what's next, with when the rug is going to be yanked out from under me and how bad it's going to hurt when I fall. Sid is so Zen. Jason has taken to calling him the Littlest Buddha, and Sid Vishnu. No wonder Jason likes him best of all our outside friends.

Of all our outside friends, if I had to pick, it's Paul Wolke I like—love, damn it—best. Must be an indication of my high self-esteem, since Paulie's the most like me. It's meaningful to me that Paulie and I have this major breakthrough, this real Annie Sullivan–Helen Keller moment, when one day I lean down to pet her and for the first time she responds to my stroke not with irritated tolerance but genuine enjoyment. She arches her back, she greets my stroke—she *gets* it. The heavens part. Cue the singing seraphim.

Could the next phase of progress be far off? Only one way to find out. Banishing memories of a freaked-out Ray Snarls as Freddy Krueger, I grab Paulie by the scruff and haul her onto my lap, stuffing her head between my thighs with one hand (what cats can't see, cats aren't afraid of), stroking her left flank with the other. She doesn't wriggle; in fact she's stiff as a taxidermy project initially, but I keep it up . . . and slowly but surely, stroke by consistent stroke, neuron by neuron, she unclenches, softens, lets go. "Let go, Paul Wolke, come on, relax," I murmur, hunching slightly to further encapsulate her with intimacy, releasing her head to reach under her chin, go for the sweet spot. She won't look at me, keeps her head ducked, but cricks her neck to meet my fingers. And that's when I feel it. Too low to hear, as if she doesn't want me to know, but the vibration is unmistakable.

Paul Wolke is purring.

point *of* no return

writing a book is like spelling *banana.* You know how to do it, you just don't know when to stop. For this book, though, I didn't expect to endlessly blather "n-a-n-a-n-a . . ." I counted on a natural narrative arc with a built-in ending—I'd start at my first feral sighting and wrap up on the last trap-neuter-return.

The thing is, in the backyard jungle, the adventure never ends. Ferals come, ferals go, ferals do strange, funny things. Once a sucker, always a sucker, so as long as kibble remains a renewable resource I could spew forever about furbag shenanigans and heartbreak. Besides, our last TNR is a moot point, a nonevent, since before Yeff Smeef's date with destiny—aka the ASPCA spay van—he goes AWOL. For good. He'd deteriorated to the point that he began to resemble the reanimated cat in the cult-gore classic *Re-Animator*, and must have ascended to that great scratching post in the sky without leaving his corpse lying around. A mess of a cat in life, in death he was tidy. Yeff Smeef, we can safely assume, dead. RIP.

For the rest of the gang things proceed fairly quietly through the summer and into the fall. Until today. Today the Mafia moves into the backyard.

I am sitting around, doing nothing, which has been my primary occupation since getting fired from my magazine job in September, when I detect a feline presence—a cat posed atop the fence post dividing the Hinkley and Hernandez properties. I wonder how long this cat has been sitting there, sizing us up, casing the joint. Indeed, I wonder *how* I notice, since the cat's black-and-tan coloring makes for excellent camouflage. Must be that creepy feeling that inches up your spine when you know—just know—someone is staring at you.

Fortunately cats are not judgmental about human appearance, since as I haven't worked in a month I've had little reason to change my sweatpants, much less fix my hair. I squint to bring the cat into focus—a *Where's Waldo* illustration of turning leaves and faded fence pickets—then gasp to myself. Axl! Axl Rose! It's Axl Rose, MIA since snow-racked, fire-beaten February, finally come home.

But why is she sitting there? Why doesn't she come to me at full gallop? Feeling like Timmy to her Lassie, I rise from my seat, heart swelling, and call to her. "Pss-pss-pss?" I venture. "Here, kitty-kitty-kitty? Yo, Axl, you dumbass furbag, it's me, Nina!"

Uh-oh. Hope this isn't less Timmy–Lassie and more Travis–Old Yeller. Can't you just hear me now, tearfully bemoaning: "Axl's got the phoby!" From this distance I cannot see whether or not the cat is foaming at the mouth, and the striped stoic does nothing to bridge the gulf between us. So, naturally, fearlessly (stupidly?), I make my way toward the back of the yard, then forge the ivy into the Hinkleys'. The cat tenses and takes off, diving like a dolphin into the brush behind the Hernandez place, leaves and twigs a susurrus chorus of crunches and snaps. The markings are all Axl, but no way is that Axl. Even raging with rabies, Axl would never run from me.

I surmise the cat to be one of those wayfaring strangers I've seen over the last half a year or so, drawn by the scent of kibble, the dangerous allure of other felines. Just passing through. Yet there he is, the next day, a sentinel in the exact same spot, levelly eyeing me. He's awfully handsome, and Jason is at work, so I repeat my siren's song, even fill a nip-sock in my efforts to entice him (hey, other desperate housewives cheat with the pool boy!). Still he spurns me. Late the next morning however, once the established feral foursome has enjoyed an AM repast and wandered off to nap sites unknown, I'm washing dishes in the kitchen and whom do I see partying down with the sock o' weed, pushing it around with his snout like a drug-addled truffle pig, rolling around and basically having a high old time.

The tiger is solid and stocky—not the dainty, fine-boned physique of Axl Rose—with a set of *cojones* the size of chestnuts. I tap the window in salutation. He drops the sock and the frivolity for a more dignified stance. We lock eyes for what seems like minutes, then he blinks once and saunters off a few feet toward one of the large plastic flowerpots that up until recently bloomed with basil. He turns his derriere to the pot—amber orbs back on me—and lifts his tail, spraying the pot to let me know, in no uncertain terms, that he has *arrived.*

Jason isn't particularly annoyed by this latest addition to the fold. Since the demise of the Vapours in July, he's gained a new "whatever" philosophy. Bands come and go, and so, apparently, do feral cats. Agreeing that the newcomer is very good-looking–a vast improvement over Yeff Smeef–Jason's the one who reasons out that the fresh feral is no doubt filling the unneutered-male spot vacated by Smeef. While Jason reminds me not to sleep on the TNR tip, he doesn't bother to protest. No doubt he suspects I've been cooing at and calling to and otherwise courting the cat in his absence.

The jury seems to be out, though, on how our regular feral family feels about the new guy. I would've thought Paulie at least would go all border guard on him, but he *is* twice her size and in full possession of his testicles. I figure they're warily curious, maybe a bit intimidated, but as far as I can tell the tom hasn't made any overt threats to their health or welfare. If anything, he's impeccably courteous. Every morning and evening when I sprinkle kibble, he shows up but hangs back, several feet from the food bowls. Sid and Nancy and Paul and Nigel dig in while the tenderfoot tucks his paws in Meat Loaf Pose and observes from respectfully afar, seeming to know his place in the pecking order.

There are only four bowls in this kibble soup kitchen, and the tom doesn't try to muscle anyone off his or her feed. Of course, his second-class-citizen status arouses my inner Jewish mother–God forbid someone should not be eating. I put a small mound of kibble on the concrete. "Come on, fella, here you go–this is for you," I say with a welcoming gesture. The cat bows his head, a paragon of polite decorum. Such knightly reticence earns him the handle Sir Douglas, after Doug Sahm, whom Jason recently introduced to our heavy rotation.

Yet it's not "Mendocino" but the opening strings of "Theme from the Godfather" that whine in my mind as I begin to suspect that this new cat may be a capo in gentleman's clothing. (There is of course precedence for this. John Gotti was widely known as the Dapper Don.) First, I realize that the instant I retire from the area, one of the ferals—most often Sid—relinquishes his bowl. Not that I see Sir Douglas behave in a menacing way. Whatever exchange transpires between Sir Douglas and Sid Vicious is too amorphous for my paltry human senses to pick up on.

Next, his moll shows up, all dressed in black. I assume she is his moll because I spy her nuzzling Sir Douglas on the nose. Then again, don't lesser mob members pay respects to the boss with a kiss? This black cat—this cohort, this underling, this henchcat—is short of tail and dull of fur. And boy is she hungry. Most cats are grazers—nosh a little here, a little there—but this cat hunkers down at a food bowl and doesn't lift her head till it's empty. This gives me a panic attack, as it further convinces me that she's female and eating for two, or three, or more. She has hit the mother lode of kibble here, and when it becomes obvious that she's sticking around I muse on potential names for her. (Remember, I don't have a job. Ruminating on cat names can consume a major part of my day.)

Since all our cats have music-oriented names, this cat should have one as well. Certainly want her to feel like she belongs. Yet I don't want to go the blatant R&B songbird route—Beyoncé, Mariah, Mary J. I'm just not into the genre, so it would feel false (although I do recall the Queen of Hip-Hop Soul was one tough chick coming up, the type to open beer bottles with her teeth). I could call her after one of the more corpulent soul divas—Etta James, Nell Carter, who by the looks of them never met a meal they didn't love. But it smacks of condescension giving a black cat a black girl's name. (For twenty years Whoopie lived as an extra-*e* namesake of Whoopi Goldberg, who floored me back in the 1980s with her breakout one-woman Broadway show. But did she—the cat, not the actress—ever feel touchy about it? After all, would I have named her Whoopie if she were another hue? You didn't see me naming Echo Shaniqua.) Finally, I dub her Dusty, for my all-time-favorite female vocalist Dusty Springfield—a skinny white chick who sang like a big black woman. Only I don't know, this cat doesn't exude that achy insecure Dusty-ness, so I reserve my right to change her name if something better occurs to me.

What Dusty exudes instead is the heart and skills of a hunter. In the course of a week she catches two mice that I'm aware of. And while Sid, Nancy, and Paul pretend not to care, Nigel is totally into this. When she tires of tossing the rodent around like a mite-infested Hacky Sack, Dusty leaves it for Nigel, who doesn't mind sloppy seconds. In fact, Nigel seems to be developing something of a schoolboy crush on Dusty, which she does nothing to discourage.

Within days I discern a strategic allegiance forming that causes me dismay. Nigel—the loneliest orphan—has joined the mob, aligning himself with Dusty and Douglas. The six ferals are now in two distinct camps, and the music in my head segues to the score of *West Side Story.* Except forget Sharks and Jets, it's the Feline Mafia versus the Sunset Minis. As always, Sir Douglas keeps his paws clean (a Teflon don as well as a dapper one), but it's not unusual for me to see Dusty and Nigel ganging up on Paul, chasing her up Big Missy the maple. Or they'll run her under this sheet of discarded tarpaper that leans against our remains of fence, then each take an entrance, making it impossible for Paul to escape.

Occasionally I'll go outside to scold Dusty and Nigel for bullying, but I know Paul Wolke can handle herself. It's Sid I'm worried about. The appearance of the Mafia felines has been messing with him big-time. Neutering really does wussify a male, and since Sidney lacks the testosterone to stand up for himself, I fear for his self-esteem. Worse, I think he's becoming depressed. I rarely see him roosting on the roof of the cat house anymore. Instead, Sir Doug has taken up residence inside, and Dusty sits on top. Sid has begun to keep irregular hours, showing up late for meals. When he does enter the yard, Douglas will give him an icy stare, and Dusty will outright run him off. And now days will pass without my seeing hide nor hair of Sid.

This has put a small, dull, ever-present pang in my solar plexus that can only be relieved by a Sid sighting. Except the next time I see Sid, it is nothing but his silhouette against an indigo sky, and my dull pang is replaced by full-on paroxysm.

Ashley has formed a new band, and tonight's their debut gig at a Lower East Side barroom. Whoo-hoo! Big doings! I doff my sweats and put an actual skirt on; I scrunch product into my frizz and festoon my eyelashes and go through all kinds of feminine primp machinations for the first time in more than a month. (It's like riding a bicycle—you don't forget how.) Alert the media: Nina Malkin is leaving the house. And it's not for an ice cream run. Watch out, world, I'm going into the city!

Before making my reentrance into polite rock 'n' roll society, I do what I always do: feed the cats. Feed the inside cats. Feed the outside cats. Do a feral head count. No sign of Sidney. It's been more than twenty-four hours now, so I shout him out. "Si-iiid! Sidney? Dinner! Come on, Sid!" I don't expect an answer.

Imagine my shock when I get one. In the form of a loud meow. "Sid? Sid, what the—where *are* you?" I call queasily at the too-balmy autumn evening air. Another meow in reply, drawn out and pitiful. I tromp around the twilit yard in my girl shoes and fishnet hose with increasingly anxious cries for Sidney to show himself, but I hear no rustle in the underbrush, no pitter-patter of little paws. And I see nothing remotely furry.

That's because I'm looking in the wrong place. I'm looking down. At the next miserable meow, I backpedal a few paces and look up. And up . . . and up. There, all alone on a Fifth Avenue rooftop, against that purplish sky with its sliver of moon and sporadic stars and the unceasing airplanes of the LaGuardia flight path, is a small blob with two triangular points on top. The blob is yowling. I clutch my chest. "SID!"

Racing into the house, I holler for Jason, who hurriedly heeds my alarm. I grab his hand, haul him outside, and point. "It's Sid," I say.

"Sid? Where?"

"Sid!" I holler, and the blob responds, and Jason sees.

"Oh, Jesus!" Jason says with a twinge of admiration. After all, it couldn't have been easy getting up there. How the hell *did* he get up there? More important, how will he get down? He wouldn't be screaming his head off if he knew the answer. Jason and I discuss strategies. It's a very brief discussion. We don't own a ladder nearly that tall, and are out of ideas.

"What goes up must come down," he philosophizes.

"Yeah, well, I'm going to the avenue," I say and, taking the nylon cat carrier, a pair of work gloves, and a flashlight—talk about imaginative fashion accessories—hit the street.

I know what roof Sid is on—the roof of New York & Company, a down-market women's clothing store. I know this, spatially challenged as I am, because looming large next to Sid's tiny silhouette is the air-conditioning unit that malfunctioned half the summer, its constant squeaky racket prompting Jason to bring it to the attention of New York & Company management. What I don't know is what I'll do or say to gain roof access—somehow I doubt the typical cashier or shopgirl will say, "Sure, honey, you go on up there and get your little cat." As it turns out, this isn't an issue. New York & Company closed ten minutes ago.

Payless Shoes and Foot Locker have also pulled their shutters for the night, but the street entrance to the dance studio above Foot Locker is unlocked. Stepping over the bundled figure nodding in the foyer, I take the flight of stairs to the dance studio and sheepishly tell the lady at the desk that I think my cat is on the roof—would she mind if I went up and checked? She wouldn't! Great!

It takes a fair amount of elbow grease to shove the two bolts locking the roof door, but I get it open. Tempting vertigo, I walk to the edge and gaze down about twenty feet onto the roof of New York & Company. It is then that I realize my folly. What am I thinking—just jump down, scoop up Sid, throw him in the carrier, sling the carrier across my back, scale the brick wall . . . Crazy cat lady, yes. Catwoman, sadly, no.

Back on the avenue—a brainstorm! What is the closest a mere mortal comes to a superhero? A firefighter, of course. I flash on a Norman Rockwell scene of kindly fireman rescuing tree-stuck kitten, and urbanize it for my purposes. Okay, how does one get into a firehouse? One rings the bell. Soon enough a firefighter who looks as if he's stepped directly from the pages of a hunk-of-the-month calendar—strawberry-blond close-cropped curls, twinkling kindly blue eyes, roses in his cheeks, dimple in his chin, muscles on his muscles—answers the bell. He has half a sandwich—a cheese sandwich, I believe—in one hand. Norman Rockwell couldn't have rendered him better! I'm saved.

With some embarrassment I tell the hunky firefighter my plight, and he is sympathetic. He wishes he could help, but he's the only one in the firehouse. The other guys are out, you know, fighting a fire. I know he's not giving me a line, because not only do I see no other firefighters milling about, I see no fire trucks, either.

Distraught, the pang in my solar plexus spawning a thud in my temporal lobes, I shuffle home. "Like you said," I tell Jason: "What goes up must come down."

Except by next morning, it doesn't come down. It simply gets louder. Jason and I gather our gear—carrier, trap, work gloves, tuna fish, can opener, your basic rudiments of cat nabbing—to pay a friendly visit to New York & Company. The managers are Julie, a plump, middle-aged woman with spidery mascara, and Derien, a thin, good-looking young guy with dreadlocks.

"The air conditioner again?" Julie asks with a tepid smile, recognizing Jason.

"Uh, no, actually . . ."

Julie and Derien are both very nice. Not nice enough to grant us roof access, however. Derien will have to contact the main office for permission. Fortunately he gets it, and calls us within the hour. Back we go to New York & Company, gear in tow like a feline SWAT team, while Derien leads the way up a steep ladder to the roof.

Plan A is for me to go on the roof and hail Sid; when he beelines for me, relieved to see his rescuer, I open the carrier and he climbs in—mission accomplished. Plan B involves the likelihood of Sid not being so accommodating—we bait the trap and return tomorrow. I start searching the roof, pss-pss-pssing. There's Sid, crouched and mournful in a pile of curling brown leaves. I hunker down. "Sid . . . ? C'mere, Sid . . . ," I beckon. Sid doesn't move. I approach him in a way that would make Monty Python's Ministry of Silly Walks but Sid fails to see what's so funny. He tears off. Plan B.

The following morning I stop at a local bakery for a pound of cookies. I pull out the bottle of Cold Duck that has been languishing in our fridge. The Cold Duck had been a gift, and since I cannot imagine who actually drinks Cold Duck, I presume it had been regifted to us. It is about to be regifted again. Jason and I go press goodies and gratitude on Julie and Derien, and Derien shows us once more to the roof. Our prayers have been answered. Sid has been snagged.

If it was tricky getting the empty cage up the steep ladder in a murky passageway, it's even trickier doing the descent, feral on board, but we manage. Back in our yard, we spring the latch and Sid takes off, mortified.

Jason and I watch him go. I couldn't possibly love my husband more than I do at this moment. He has gone above and beyond the call of duty. He deserves a medal of valor. He is truly wonderful. I hug him and tell him how truly wonderful he is, how grateful I am.

"No big deal," he says modestly. "It was an experience. And one thing's for sure, we'll never have to go through that again."

Until about four days later.

It's not déjà vu, it's not a bad dream—it's real, it's happening. Again! That stupid little furbag! This time we discover Sid's whereabouts in the morning, and lucky for me, Jason isn't working today. Sid's second rooftop escapade is a calamity on so many levels, but the worst of it is the nice people at New York & Company. We go in with our gear and head for the small management office behind a display of affordable handbags. Julie's there by herself.

"Hey, Julie, guess what? Heh-heh-heh. He's up there again? Mind if we trot on up with our trap?"

It's not that Julie minds, it's that she doesn't have the keys to the roof. Can we come back at one, when Derien is there? Of course we can. We do. But Derien crosses his arms over his chest. Derien is adamant. No way. He blames the home office, saying they told him they can't continue taking risks with lunatics on their roof. Lunatics are a liability; we belong on the ground. Hysteria rising, I make unqualified statements about how it's illegal to knowingly allow an animal to starve to death, how this is an animal rights violation. I threaten how PETA and the ASPCA will hear about this, as well as New York Attorney General Eliot Spitzer and Brooklyn Borough President Marty Markowitz, whom I know personally (a bald-faced lie). Derien isn't buying it. He's a sharp dresser and he already got soot on one pair of trousers this week over some dumb cat.

Shit!

I am beside myself, but inside Jason's cranium the gears are turning. He gets an idea and tries to break it down for me, but I am way beyond reason. I tell him I'll do whatever he says, and he begins gathering supplies. Apparently there will be rope involved. Our first stop is the dance studio, which is closed, but the law office next door is open, and we attempt to explain our situation to the secretary.

"Your *what* is *where?*" she says. "You want to do what!"

Several attempts later she takes our plea to the attorney, and returns with the message: "You want to go on the roof, you got to talk to Foot Locker." Now, that's an attorney for you—absolving himself of responsibility.

Much to our good fortune, the manager of Foot Locker is both busy and laid-back. He doesn't need us to draw him a picture, he doesn't care why we want to go on the roof—he just says okay.

Okay. This is good. Now we are on the roof of Foot Locker. We are opening a can of tuna fish; we are placing the can in the trap. We are setting the trap. We are tying the rope to the handle of the trap, and we are carefully, very carefully, lowering the trap twenty feet or so from the roof of Foot Locker to the roof of New York & Company. At four o'clock we are coming back. And we are carefully, very carefully, hauling up a trap full of Sidney.

If I thought I couldn't possibly love Jason more than I did four days ago, I was wrong. I love him far more now. I love him even more that evening when, under cover of darkness, he takes a saw and a ladder and trespasses into the yard of the recently renovated former fire zone next door. There he spends an hour and a half cutting down the limb of a tree he surmises provides Sid access to the New York & Company roof. Keep your firemen. Your Spider-Men, your Supermen, your Batmen, your Incredible Hulks. I don't need them. I have Jason Shealy Stutts. He is the best man a crazy cat lady could ever hope to find. He is *my* man. And he is my hero.

Once we get Sid back in the yard the second time, we spring him and watch him bound off like a white-tailed deer. We never see him again.

I cannot help it. I cry over Sid. The problem is, as it always is when a feral vanishes, I don't know when to start crying, because it's hard to gauge when the hoping he'll return settles into the knowing he's gone, really gone. This makes my crying intermittent, and foolhardy, and unsatisfying.

It's Halloween morning. I bait the trap. The charisma of the tuna can calls to Dusty, and once inside she goes so berserk that the cage rocks violently for fifteen frightening seconds. I bring her to the vet. When I call to find out if it's okay to pick her up, they tell me Dusty is male. Whatever. I bring *him* home. Put *him* in the bathtub. Jason decides we should call him Richard Wayne (in homage to the human being who rose to prominence with the moniker Little Richard). I say okay. Whatever, whatever—I don't want to care.

It's Halloween afternoon in a neighborhood bursting with little kids, but the trick-or-treating happens on Fifth Avenue. It's safer for kids to go store-to-store than house-to-house. You never know what monster lurks behind the door to a house, what horrors await inside. In Sunset kids learn suspicion at an early age.

Up on the avenue, it's an unofficial Halloween parade. Parents dress up and wander alongside sugar-manic children, keeping a watchful eye. Many costumes are homemade. A lot are Latin Gothic, very Day of the Dead—devils and skeletons, plus a preponderance of vampires, the dark lip pencil and heavy eyeliner of the *chola* look one and the same with the Goth look. Last year, our first Halloween in Sunset, Jason and I just got caught up in the cavalcade by chance; we weren't prepared with excessive makeup or kooky clothes. Today we speak of joining the procession proper—we are no longer Sunset neophytes, we are of the community now. I contemplate a long black dress and Morticia *maquillage*, and Jason is game to wear his black felt derby and carry a pitchfork.

But I don't know. Though I've always enjoyed Halloween, this is the time of year we lost my dad, so late October pretty much sucks for me now. Most times, when I think of my dad, the memories are fond and the feelings are good—wistful, but good. I think about how well he and Jason would have gotten on, playing country songs on guitar, taking off on photography jaunts. I can see my dad visiting our house, kibitzing on projects, making us aware of what's most likely to fall apart next. He'd canoodle with Iggy and Echo, and he'd sit with me outside on the milk crates (I busted the bucket a while ago), trying to win over Paulie and the gang.

It's only around Halloween that my memories and feelings are too much choked by a selfish sense of loss, by fear and regret. So as the shadows lengthen, I just can't do it, cannot muster the energy for the candy, for the crowd.

I sit in the house. Then I do what I always do: I feed the cats. Feed the inside cats. Feed the outside cats. I linger in the yard. It's still warm out, no jacket required, and this unnerves me. When the cold comes, it will come with a bang, with a *Gotcha!* It will not "grow" cold like a neglected plate of spaghetti; I will wake up one day and it will be there.

I want Paul Wolke to live in the house. No, you don't understand: I *want* Paul *Wolke* to *live* in the *house.* Jason would be against it. He won't want to do it to Iggy and Echo; it would be unfair to upset their privileged existence. He won't want to pan for extra poop, either. Still, I think I might be able to convince him. I could probably get Iggy and Echo to forgive me, too, and eventually accept Paul Wolke as a little sister—Echo mostly white, Iggy mostly black, Paulie equal parts black and white. How cute they'd all look together.

I scoop Paulie up and put her on my lap. She's not into it—she squirms away. Therein lies the trouble with my scheme. Paul Wolke has her own agenda; she follows her own set of feline rules that I'll never comprehend. But I know this: Paul Wolke doesn't want to live in the house. There are no trees in the house, no squirrels. The house has walls. She doesn't want walls; she doesn't want boundaries. Jason has taken to calling her Wolke, Brooklyn Ranger, for a reason. She may not ever want to be wet, she may not ever want to be cold—and soon it will be cold—but Paul *Wolke* doesn't *want* to *live* in the *house*. And this is about Paul Wolke. This is so not about me.

appendix

got ferals?

If this book has inspired you to do your part to reduce the feral cat overpopulation problem—and not, you know, run screaming in the opposite direction—you don't have to DIY TNR. There are people who will help. To find a feral cat advocacy group in your area, start by plugging "feral cats" and your state into a search engine. Also try your local Humane Society or ASPCA. Check out the list below:

NATIONAL

Humane Society of the United States (www.hsus.org)

SPAY USA (www.spayusa.org)

Alley Cat Allies (www.alleycat.org)

Neighborhood Cats (www.neighborhoodcats.org)

BY STATE

California

(Los Angeles) The Feral Cat Alliance (www.feralcatalliance.org)

(Santa Cruz) Project Purr (www.projectpurr.org)

Colorado

(Denver) Rocky Mountain Alley Cat Alliance (www.rmaca.com)

Connecticut

(New Haven) Greater New Haven Cat Project

(www.orgsites.com/ct/gnhcp)

Florida

(Miami) The Cat Network (www.thecatnetwork.org)

(Tampa) Fix and Feed Feline Feral, Inc. (www.fffelineferal.com)

Georgia

(Northwest Georgia) The Sterile Feral, Inc.
(www.thesterileferal.org)

Hawaii

(Honolulu) Cat Friends (www.hicatfriends.org)

Illinois

(Champaign) Champaign Area Trap Spay Neuter and Adoption
Program (www.catsnap.org)

Massachusetts

(Statewide) Massachusetts Animal Coalition
(www.massanimalcoalition.org)

Michigan

(Ann Arbor) TLC/For the Love of Cats (tlconline.org)

North Carolina

(Raleigh) Operation Catnip (www.operationcatnip.org)

Oregon

(Satewide) Pet Over-Population Prevention Advocates, Inc.
(POPPA) (www.poppainc.org/spayneuter.asp)

Pennsylvania

(Central Pennsylvania) Paws of PA (www.pawsofpa.org)

Tennessee

(Knoxville) Knoxville Feral Cat Friends (www.knoxvilleferalcat
friends.org)

Texas

(Austin) Austin Feral Cats (www.austinferalcats.org)

Virginia

(Arlington) Metro Ferals (www.metroferals.org

acknowledgments

i would like to thank all

the people who've lent support and assistance to this feral adventure. Byran Kortis and Meredith Weiss of Neighborhood Cats, Jude Lassow-Sunden of Muffin's Pet Connection, Rosemary Padua Kassel Stolzenberg, Gini Sikes and David Conrad, Matt Morgan and Amy Nathanson, Ashley DeVries, Faye Chiu, everyone at the Animal Clinic of Bay Ridge and the Prospect Park Clinic, Joe Hinkley and family for being such tolerant neighbors, and Mexicana Car Service. I would also like to thank my agent, the indomitable Laura Dail, and my editors, Ann Treistman and Maureen Graney, for their caring touch and guidance. Finally, much as I may blather, I have no words to accurately express my gratitude to Jason Shealy Stutts—I'll have to do so in kibble . . . uh, kisses.

An Unlikely Cat Lady